Joy to the World

Dedication

To my daughter Susannah, whose pregnancy and subsequent birth of Jemima Josephine accompanied the writing of this book

Joy
to the
World

Preaching
the
Christmas
story

Paul Beasley-Murray

Inter-Varsity Press

Inter-Varsity Press
38 De Montfort Street, Leicester LE1 7GP, England
Email: ivp@uccf.org.uk
Website: www.ivpbooks.com

British Library Cataloguing in Publication Data
A catalogue record for this book is available from the British Library.

ISBN-13: 978-1-84474-081-9
ISBN-10: 1-84474-081-1

Set in Monotype Dante 10.5/13pt

Typeset in Great Britain by Servis Filmsetting Ltd, Manchester
Printed and bound in Great Britain by Creative Print and Design (Wales),
Ebbw Vale

*Inter-Varsity Press is the publishing division of the Universities and
Colleges Christian Fellowship (formerly the Inter-Varsity Fellowship), a
student movement linking Christian Unions in universities and colleges
throughout Great Britain, and a member movement of the International
Fellowship of Evangelical Students. For more information about local
and national activities write to UCCF, 38 De Montfort Street, Leicester
LE1 7GP, email us at email@uccf.org.uk, or visit the UCCF website at
www.uccf.org.uk.*

Contents

Acknowledgments

I wish to acknowledge the generosity of the deacons and members of Central Baptist Church, Victoria Road South, Chelmsford, in their kindness in giving me time every year for study and writing. Without that thoughtful provision there is no way in which I as the senior minister of a busy town-centre church could ever have written this book.

I wish too to acknowledge the help of Philip Duce, Theological Books Editor at IVP, for his guidance and assistance; as also the hospitality of my friend Ursula Franklin, in whose home a good deal of the initial writing took place.

Above all I wish to acknowledge the love and support of my wife, Caroline.

Paul Beasley-Murray

Introduction

Yet another Christmas marathon is over, thank God! And what a marathon it was, with one carol service following another. Although from a strict liturgical point of view, Christmas doesn't begin until Christmas Day itself, in practice Christmas and Advent merge into one another, with the result that whereas most churches tend to confine their singing of Easter hymns to Easter Day, Christmas carols are sung for weeks on end. What's more, along with the singing of the carols goes the preaching of the Christmas story, which reaches a crescendo on 'Christmas Sunday' (i.e. the Sunday before Christmas), Christmas Eve and Christmas Day.

For any pastor, just to survive one Christmas is demanding. But to survive one Christmas after another and still have something fresh to say is a true challenge. I speak here from experience. For I have served in two churches for twenty-five years: I was in my first church for thirteen years, and then, after a break as a theological college principal, have been in my present church for some twelve years. It is not easy, year after year, to find new approaches to the Christmas story.

To my mind the secret to preaching at Christmas – as indeed to preaching at any time of the year – is to be found in expository preaching. For expository preaching enables the preacher to remain fresh. When we conscientiously expound God's Word, we discover that we are always finding new truths to impart. But left to our own devices, we soon run out of bright ideas. In the words of the great Scottish preacher, James Stewart, 'The preacher who expounds his own limited stock of ideas becomes deadly wearisome at last. The preacher who expounds the Bible has endless variety at his disposal.

For no two texts say exactly the same thing.'[1] What is true of preaching in general is, I believe, also true when it comes to preaching the message of Christmas. It is this belief in expository preaching which underlies this book.

Needless to say, expository preaching involves more than simply having a text. For the preacher it involves studying the text. In the first place such study will involve an engagement with the text itself. For those who are able, this will mean reading the passage in its original Hebrew or Greek. It will certainly mean comparing one English version with another to gain the various nuances present in the text. It will also involve seeing how God has guided his people in the past in understanding the text (see 2 Pet. 1:20). This in turn will involve reading several commentaries on the passage in question. Only then can we move on to consider how we might apply God's Word to our congregations creatively, sensitively and relevantly.

Effective preaching, however, involves more than study and reflection. It also involves the hard work of shaping. Or to put it another way: there are three stages to preparing a sermon: first, listening to the voice of God in Scripture; secondly, listening to the voices in the world around; and then, fixing the listening process in a way which enables people to hear clearly what God would say to them through the preacher.

Needless to say, there is no one God-given way in which sermons must be shaped. But shape there must be. Rather than engage in a leisurely discursive ramble, the preacher needs to have a structure which serves to ram home the points that need to be made on the basis of the passage in question. Structure gives clarity to preaching. Napoleon is said to have had three commands for his messengers: 'Be clear! Be clear! Be clear!' Preachers, too, need to be crystal clear. Our congregations need to be able to leave the service under no illusion about what was said. Structure, too, gives purpose and power to preaching. It enables preachers to develop an argument and apply it so that there is only one conclusion. For preachers, like barristers, are advocates: they are seeking a verdict.

———————

1. James S. Stewart, *Preaching* (London: Teach Yourself Books: English Universities Press, 1955), p. 96.

If ever there is a time when clear gospel preaching is required, it is at Christmas. For Christmas, at least in early twenty-first century Britain, is increasingly the one time in the year when many non-Christians are prepared to go to church. Indeed, according to a survey in 2003, as many as four out of ten adults were hoping to attend a Christmas service. Considering that less than one in ten people in Britain are regular church-goers, that is some statistic. It also means that Christmas is a great opportunity for gospel preaching.

The principal aim of this particular book is to help preachers in their God-given task of telling the story of how God sent his Son to be the Saviour of the world. But it is not just a book for preachers. I hope it will be of stimulus to listeners too.

Two other comments need to be made. First, the English text I have adopted is the New Revised Standard Version (NRSV) of the Bible. In many evangelical churches the preferred text is the New International Version (NIV). In my own church we have adopted the Good News Bible (GNB) for the simple reason that it is the most accessible of translations for the ordinary person. However, to my mind there is little doubt that the NRSV is the best study text, as is evidenced by its adoption in most universities and theological colleges as its set English text. Indeed, the NRSV has become the recommended text for use with the Church of England's *Common Worship* service book.

Secondly, I cannot claim originality for all I have written. I have naturally consulted the commentaries and other scholarly studies; and in particular I have drawn upon *The Birth of the Messiah* by Raymond E. Brown.[2] Over the years I have also read a good deal of popular exposition. However, my study originally was with a view to preaching, and there are no footnotes in a sermon! The result is that I have not always kept track of where some of my ideas or quotations have come. I trust that readers will forgive me if they deem that I have not given credit where credit is due.

---

2. Raymond E. Brown, *The Birth of the Messiah: A Commentary on the Infancy Narratives in Matthew and Luke* (London: Geoffrey Chapman, 1977).

1   The Good News according to Matthew

The first two chapters of Matthew's Gospel provide a rich resource for the preacher at Christmas. Inevitably, the focus of attention is on Matthew's account of the birth of Jesus and of the visit of the wise men. However, even the apparently boring genealogy of Jesus, as also the grisly story of the massacre of the children, throw light on the child who came to save.

Matthew's account of the birth of Jesus is very different from that of Luke. Whereas in Luke's Gospel Mary is at the centre of the attention, in Matthew the focus is very much on Joseph. Whether or not this is due to Matthew's account being ultimately dependent upon the memories of Joseph, is a matter of debate. However, it is clear that Matthew is drawing upon traditions quite separate from those known to Luke. For some, the differences between the two sets of traditions create problems; however, from our perspective the very differences may well be viewed as an argument for the underlying truth of the story being told.

The genealogy of Jesus the Messiah (Matt. 1:1–17)

An account of the genealogy of Jesus the Messiah, the son of David, the son of Abraham.

Abraham was the father of Isaac, and Isaac the father of Jacob, and Jacob the father of Judah and his brothers, and Judah the father of Perez and Zerah by Tamar, and Perez the father of Hezron, and Hezron the father of Aram, and Aram the father of Aminadab, and Aminadab the father of Nahshon, and Nahshon the father of Salmon, and Salmon the father of Boaz by Rahab, and Boaz the father of Obed by Ruth, and Obed the father of Jesse, and Jesse the father of King David.

And David was the father of Solomon by the wife of Uriah, and Solomon the father of Rehoboam, and Rehoboam the father of Abijah, and Abijah the father of Asaph, and Asaph the father of Jehoshaphat, and Jehoshaphat the father of Joram, and Joram the father of Uzziah, and Uzziah the father of Jotham, and Jotham the father of Ahaz, and Ahaz the father of Hezekiah, and Hezekiah the father of Manasseh, and Manasseh the father of Amos, and Amos the father of Josiah, and Josiah the father of Jechoniah and his brothers, at the time of the deportation to Babylon.

And after the deportation to Babylon: Jechoniah was the father of Salathiel, and Salathiel the father of Zerubbabel, and Zerubbabel the father of Abiud, and Abiud the father of Eliakim, and Eliakim the father of Azor, and Azor the father of Zadok, and Zadok the father of Achim, and Achim the father of Eliud, and Eliud the father of Eleazar, and Eleazar the father of Matthan, and Matthan the father of Jacob, and Jacob the father of Joseph the husband of Mary, of whom Jesus was born, who is called the Messiah.

So all the generations from Abraham to David are fourteen generations; and from David to the deportation to Babylon, fourteen generations; and from the deportation to Babylon to the Messiah, fourteen generations.

Son of Abraham, David, and of the Exile

Tracing one's family tree is a popular pastime today, and understandably so. For as we trace back our past, we discover that our family history is not 'as dry as dust', but is made up of a host of colourful characters. Family trees were also popular with the Jews, and the Old Testament contains many a genealogical list. These genealogies were a means of establishing significance, legitimacy and identity. It is therefore not surprising that Matthew, as also Luke, provides Jesus with a family tree.

Matthew begins his Gospel with the genealogy of Jesus. For most modern readers this is a turn-off, and we are tempted to skip on to the story of the birth of Jesus itself. But to do so would be to miss Matthew's purpose. Through providing a family tree of Jesus, Matthew is informing us about the identity of the one whose life, death and resurrection he features throughout his Gospel. To make it crystal clear he begins with an opening summary statement: 'An account of the genealogy of Jesus the Messiah, the son of David, the son of Abraham' (1:1).

All Jews could trace their ancestry back to Abraham, some could even trace their ancestry back to David, but Jesus alone is the Christ, 'the Messiah'. In some versions of the Bible the word 'Christ' is treated as just a name, and so they translate this opening verse as: 'An account of the genealogy of Jesus Christ, the son of David, the son of Abraham.' But although Matthew uses the Greek word *Christos*, almost certainly he is using it as a title. So when at the end of the family tree Matthew finally reaches Joseph, he describes him as 'the husband of Mary, of whom Jesus was born, who is the Messiah' (1:16).

The structure of Jesus' family tree is significant. Matthew quite deliberately groups Jesus' ancestors into three sections of fourteen: 'So all the generations from Abraham to David are fourteen generations; and from David to the deportation to Babylon, fourteen generations; and from the deportation to Babylon to the Messiah, fourteen generations' (1:17). A careful reading of the family tree reveals that this is an artificial structure.

For instance, his genealogy is incomplete, because at times he jumps several generations. Had Matthew been simply in the business of listing every one of Jesus' ancestors, then he would have also included between Joram and Uzziah the names of Ahaziah, Jehoash and Amaziah (see 1 Chr. 3:11–12) and between Josiah and Jeconiah the name of Jehoiakim (see 1 Chr. 3:15–16). But he omitted, and almost certainly deliberately so, these four names – perhaps because all these four Davidic kings were for varying reasons put under a curse; or perhaps because he wanted to get down to the symbolic number fourteen. Matthew's use of the term 'father', therefore, is occasionally somewhat loose. But this use is not surprising: the underlying

Greek word was sufficiently elastic to have the sense of 'ancestor' rather than 'immediate father'.

Another so-called discrepancy is that a close counting of Matthew's three groups reveals that the third group contains only thirteen sons, unless perhaps we are also to count the name of Mary.

For some these discrepancies are a cause of concern. However, we need to be aware that Matthew was not interested in writing a 'pure' history as such; rather, he was much more interested in writing a 'Gospel'. For Matthew, like the other three Gospel writers, was a 'propagandist' in the sense that he had a particular message to put over. This is not to say that he had no interest in historical truth. Rather, Matthew drew upon historical sources to support his case. So here in his presentation of Jesus' family tree Matthew is making a theological point: Jesus is not just one member in an ongoing family, but he is the goal of the whole family. Hence the arrangement of the family tree into three groups of fourteen names. Some scholars, noting that the numerical values of the Hebrew consonants in David's name (*dwd*) add up to the number fourteen (4 + 6 + 4), have suggested that this particular arrangement is intended to underline the fact that Jesus is the Son of David. An alternative suggestion is that the three groups of fourteen are in effect six groups of seven names: since in Jewish thinking the number seven was one of the most powerful symbolic numbers, to be born at the beginning of the seventh seven in the sequence is clearly to be the climax. Whichever option we go for, the conclusion is the same: Jesus is the Messiah, the one for whom Israel has been waiting for so many years.

Before we look more closely at Jesus' family tree, we need perhaps to deal with the issue that the genealogy found here in Matthew's Gospel is different in quite a number of ways from the genealogy found in Luke's Gospel (Luke 3:23–38).

Some of these differences are not of great importance: for instance, it is neither here nor there that Luke traces Jesus' family tree in a reverse order from that of Matthew; theologically, it is significant that Luke traces Jesus' family tree back to Adam 'the son of God' (Luke 3:38), whereas Matthew only goes as far back as Abraham, but this is simply Luke's way of emphasizing Jesus' universal significance, and is not therefore a factual difference.

More problematic is that Luke traces the messianic line through

David's son Nathan, instead of through Solomon, with the result that all the names from David to Joseph (Luke 3:23–31) are different from those found in Matthew. The result is that in Matthew's Gospel the father of Joseph is Jacob (Matt. 1:16), whereas in Luke's Gospel the father of Joseph is Eli or Heli (the spelling is dependent upon whether or not one adopts the Greek 'breathing') (Luke 1:23). One common solution to this problem is to suggest that Matthew presents us with Joseph's family tree, while Luke presents us effectively with Mary's family tree. It may be, for instance, that Mary had no brothers, so that on her marriage to Joseph, her father Heli (Eli), in line with a biblical tradition concerned with the maintenance of the family line where there was no male heir (see Ezra 2:61 = Neh. 7:63), adopted Joseph as his own son, with the result that Matthew therefore gives Joseph's ancestry by birth, and Luke gives Joseph's ancestry by adoption. Whatever be the truth, one thing is certain: neither Matthew nor Luke cared much about the identity of the biological grandfather of Jesus; their chief concern was theological, to show that Jesus was 'the son of David' and 'the son of Abraham' (Matt. 1:1) or in the case of Luke that he was 'the son of Adam' . . . the 'son of God' (Luke 3:38).

So we return to Matthew and his genealogy. Matthew's first group of fourteen names (1:2–6a) centres around the fact that Jesus is 'the son of Abraham'. At first sight this appears to suggest that Jesus was therefore a true Jew. However, almost certainly this is not the emphasis that Matthew is seeking to make. We need to be mindful that in the Old Testament Abraham is more than a founding father of the nation of Israel: he is also the one in whom 'all the families of the earth shall be blessed' (see Gen. 12:3). Although Matthew's Gospel is the most Jewish of Gospels, Matthew does not want to depict Jesus just as a Jewish Messiah, but rather to show that he is the Saviour of the world. This is undoubtedly one reason why Matthew included the story of the magi (2:1–12): the magi who came to worship him, are representative of the Gentile world. And, of course, Matthew ends his Gospel with the Great Commission, where Jesus instructs his disciples to go 'and make disciples of all nations' (28:19). As 'son of Abraham', Jesus has universal significance.

For the preacher this emphasis on Jesus as the son of Abraham in whom there is blessing for all is an important point for development.

It means, for instance, that in Jesus there is not simply blessing for Jew and for Gentile, but also for black and for white, for the privileged and the underprivileged.

There is another aspect to Abraham that the preacher may wish to develop. Abraham was a man of faith (see Rom. 4:1–13; Gal. 3:6–9; Jas 2:21–23). As the writer of the Hebrews reminds us: 'By faith Abraham obeyed when he was called to set out for a place that he was to receive as an inheritance; and he set out, not knowing where he was going' (Heb. 11:8). Abraham in obedience to God's call exercised what in effect was 'blind faith': when he set out from Haran he had no certainties upon which to rest his faith, for at that stage in his experience God was to a large extent the Great Unknown. However, the point worth developing is that in Jesus Abraham's faith in God finds fulfilment and definition. For Jesus came to reveal God to us, and in so doing he calls us to place our faith in the God and Father of our Lord Jesus Christ, and so discover the blessing of sins forgiven and life eternal. This then is the good news: Jesus, as the son of Abraham, wants to be everybody's Saviour.

Jesus too is the 'Son of David'. It is around David that Matthew's second group of names (1:6b–11) centres. David was Israel's greatest king; a point perhaps underlined by Matthew in that in his genealogy David alone of Jesus' royal ancestors is given the title of 'King' (1:6). When Jews looked back in history, they looked back to the reign of David as a golden age; just as today the British look back to the reigns of Elizabeth I and of Queen Victoria as outstanding eras in their national life, when Britannia did indeed rule the waves. But the Jews didn't just look back: they also looked forward to the coming of the Messiah who would inaugurate an age even more splendid than David's. For Matthew, Jesus as 'the son of David' was the one in whom the 'messianic' promises were fulfilled. Almost certainly Matthew had in mind the words of the Lord delivered through the prophet Nathan to David: 'I will raise up your offspring after you, who shall come forth from your body, and I will establish his kingdom . . . your throne shall be established forever' (2 Sam. 7:12b–16). In turn this meant that Jesus, as 'the son of David', was the one in whom God had fulfilled his promises; he was the one in whom the longed-for golden age had come; he was the one in whom Israel's dreams had come true.

We may not dream of a Jewish Messiah, but many of us do dream of a world in which peace and justice reign; we long for a day when tears will be wiped away, when 'mourning and crying and pain will be no more' (Rev. 21:4). In this context the preacher has good news to declare: Jesus came to make our dreams come true: not narrow egotistical dreams related to personal ambition, but rather our dreams of a coming kingdom of God, where right and not might will triumph, when all will truly be well. Matthew, in describing Jesus as the son of David, is describing one who is able to make our deepest dreams come true.

Finally, Matthew's third grouping of names (1:12–16) shows that Jesus is 'the son of the Exile'. Although Matthew does not actually use this title, he does highlight the deportation of the people of Israel to Babylon (1:12, 17). If David's reign evoked memories of past greatness, the exile evoked memories of past bitterness. For then God's people had been torn from their homes, they had been transported hundreds of miles away to become the slaves of a cruel and imperious nation. It is no exaggeration to say that the Exile was a precursor of the later Holocaust. The songs with which God's people had celebrated their faith and praised their God died on their lips once they were deported to Babylon: they hung their harps upon the trees, their hearts too heavy to make music (Ps. 137:2). Jesus, as 'the son of the Exile', was a descendant of those suffering and dispossessed people. Indeed, he was not just a descendant: he knew from his own experience what suffering and dispossession were all about.

But the preacher needs to remember that Israel's history did not come to an end with the Exile. God in his goodness brought his people back to the Promised Land. The day came when they took down their harps again and sang a new song to the God of their salvation. Jesus, as 'the son of the Exile', is a pointer to the fact that with God no situation is hopeless. Indeed, the good news is that God has again intervened in human history, for in Jesus his Son he has provided us with a Saviour: one who 'will save his people from their sins' (1:21). Jesus by his coming came to bring us the freedom which really matters: freedom from sin, freedom from death. Yes, for all who put their faith in Jesus, the son of the Exile, there is freedom to live now and freedom to live with God eternally.

Listen, says Matthew, listen to this genealogy. This is no ordinary family tree. This is no mere record of biological productivity. It is a sign of God at work.

A cupboard of family skeletons

As many a presidential or prime-ministerial hopeful has discovered, most – if not all of us – have skeletons in the family cupboard. Jesus was no exception. The stories of none of the four women mentioned by Matthew in his genealogy of Jesus are stories really fit for family reading. The story of Tamar, for instance, details not just the behaviour of Onan, her brother-in-law, who whenever he had sex ejaculated on to the ground, but also the behaviour of Tamar herself, who went out of her way to have sex with her father-in-law (Gen. 38). Rahab was no better: for whereas Tamar pretended to be 'on the game', Rahab was a professional prostitute, offering herself to all and sundry (Josh. 2:1). Although past commentators have tried to gloss over this unpalatable fact, with the NIV's alternative reading describing her as 'innkeeper', there seems little doubt that Rahab ran a brothel. Then there was Ruth, a truly admirable daughter-in-law, yet also a woman who was not afraid to chase her man. What exactly went on at midnight on the threshing floor, when Ruth 'uncovered his feet, and lay down' (Ruth 3:7)? The story is full of euphemisms and double-meanings, which suggest that Ruth probably seduced Boaz. As for Bathsheba, termed by Matthew 'the wife of Uriah', while it may be true that she had little option in resisting the advances of the king, she may well have been asking for trouble in bathing in a place where she could be observed (2 Sam. 11:2).[1]

Since, as we have seen, Matthew could be selective when it came to drawing up the names of Jesus' ancestors, why did he include these four characters, all of whom had somewhat shady sex lives? The early church father Jerome believed the inclusion of these four women points to the fact that Jesus came to save sinners. However, it

---

1. So, for instance, A. W. Hertzberg, *1 & 2 Samuel* (ET London: SCM Press, 1964), p. 309. However, Mary J. Evans, *The Message of Samuel* (Leicester: IVP, 2004), p. 209, would have us believe that 'There is nothing in the text to justify the picture of Bathsheba as behaving deliberately in an alluring manner and setting out to seduce the unworldly and innocent David'!

is not clear whether Jesus' contemporaries regarded these women as archetypal sinners: the rabbis, for instance, were at times quite complimentary about them. Luther believed their inclusion was due to the fact that they were all Gentiles: Tamar was an Aramaean (Jubilees 41:1), Rahab was a Canaanite, Ruth a Moabite, and Bathsheba was married to Uriah the Hittite. However, although Matthew was keen to show that Jesus was the Saviour of the world, there is no certainty that this thought was behind his inclusion of the women. It appears that in early Judaism all four women were accepted as honoured proselytes.

Bearing in mind that Matthew ends his genealogy with Mary, it is more likely that Matthew included these four women because in a differing ways they prefigured Mary's relationship with Joseph. In each case there was something odd, if not scandalous, about their union with their male partners. Furthermore, in spite of the apparent 'shadiness' of their relationships, each one of them played a significant role in God's purposes. Finally, each one of them actively played a part in those purposes by at one stage or another taking a significant risk, or what we might term an 'act of faith'.

Tamar's behaviour was actually not as outrageous as it first appears. For Tamar had been wronged; under Jewish law after the death of her husband she had a right to expect one of his relatives to father a child for her. Nonetheless, she took a risk in seducing Judah: once her pregnancy was discovered she could have been stoned for her shamelessness. Like Mary, she experienced the scandal of becoming pregnant while unmarried; yet in so doing she fulfilled the purposes of God.

Rahab enters the stage of history as a prostitute (Josh. 2:1), yet she leaves it as one of faith's heroines (Heb. 11:31), for she risked her life in hiding Joshua and Caleb. Her faith was exemplified in her response to the two spies, 'According to your words, so be it' (Josh. 2:21), words which later are almost exactly duplicated by Mary in her response to the angel Gabriel: 'let it be with me according to your word' (Luke 1:38). In spite of their differences, Rahab and Mary were soul-sisters.

Ruth and Mary were also kindred souls, in the sense that for both of them their journey to Bethlehem was a journey of faith. As Mary made her way to Bethlehem, she must have wondered what the future held for her and her unborn child. Similarly, Ruth in following

Naomi to Bethlehem must have wondered what the future held for her. Humanly speaking, the prospects were far from good. Yet she abandoned her native gods and bravely declared to her mother-in-law, 'Your God' will be 'my God' (Ruth 1:16). Was her coming to Boaz by night an act of faith too? She certainly took a risk, for Boaz might have been angry rather than just surprised. Ruth and Mary were both women whose faith enabled them to show 'guts' and determination (see Ruth 1:18).

Of all the four women, perhaps Bathsheba's connection with Mary is the most tenuous. Yet there are parallels. Ambitious for her second son, Absalom, she – like Mary – experienced the pain of seeing death bringing her dreams to nothing. The cry of David was no doubt echoed in the heart of Bathsheba, and probably in the heart of Mary too: 'my son, my son . . . Would I had died instead of you, . . . my son, my son!' (2 Sam. 18:33).

All of these four women, who in one way or another prefigured Mary, had their shortcomings. And yet, in spite of their past, God in his grace used them in one way or another to fulfil his purposes. Here is a challenge for us. In what way will we be remembered? Will in future days stories be told of our faith, of our determination, of our actions and decisions which in one way or another advanced the cause of the kingdom?

So, strange as it may seem initially, these four women provide good material for preaching. In particular, they illustrate three things about God. First, God is in the business of saving sinners: even people like Tamar, who seduced her father-in-law; Rahab, who was a prostitute; Ruth, who probably seduced Boaz; and Bathsheba, who committed adultery with David. For God sent his Son 'to save his people from their sins' (1:21). Secondly, God is in the business of saving everybody: even Gentiles like Tamar, Rahab, Ruth and Bathsheba, who did not belong to God's chosen people. Jesus is good news for people of every race, colour and nation (see Matt. 8:11). Thirdly, God is in the business of surprising us all: although there was something odd, if not scandalous about their union with their partners, God used each one of these four women to play a part in fulfilling his purposes. Furthermore, as Matthew makes clear in the conclusion to his genealogy, God surprised us in the very circumstances of Jesus' birth: for instead of declaring that 'Joseph was the father of Jesus', Matthew uses instead a divine passive as he speaks of 'Mary, of whom Jesus was born' (1:16). God was at work in the birth of Jesus.

The birth of Jesus (Matt. 1:18–25)

Now the birth of Jesus the Messiah took place in this way. When his mother Mary had been engaged to Joseph, but before they lived together, she was found to be with child from the Holy Spirit. Her husband Joseph, being a righteous man and unwilling to expose her to public disgrace, planned to dismiss her quietly. But just when he had resolved to do this, an angel of the Lord appeared to him in a dream and said, 'Joseph, son of David, do not be afraid to take Mary as your wife, for the child conceived in her is from the Holy Spirit. She will bear a son, and you are to name him Jesus, for he will save his people from their sins.' All this took place to fulfil what had been spoken by the Lord through the prophet:

> *'Look, the virgin shall conceive and bear a son,*
> *and they shall name him Emmanuel',*

which means, 'God is with us.' When Joseph awoke from sleep, he did as the angel of the Lord commanded him; he took her as his wife, but had no marital relations with her until she had borne a son; and he named him Jesus.

Son of Mary, son of God

Today many people live together before they get married, whereas Mary and Joseph were in the eyes of the law 'married' but not living together. An explanation is called for. In ancient Judaism matrimonial procedures involved the taking of two steps: the first step involved a formal consent before witnesses; the second step involved the man taking his bride into his home. In our culture we would speak of 'engagement' and 'marriage', but such terms can be unhelpful when it comes to understanding the relationship between Joseph and Mary. 'Betrothal' in the time of Jesus was a far more serious business than our custom of 'engagement'. From the moment the girl was betrothed, she was the man's 'wife': if her 'husband' died during the period of the betrothal, she was regarded as a widow; if she committed adultery, she could be punished; and the only way in which the marriage contract entered upon at the moment of betrothal could be annulled was by divorce. At that time betrothal took place usually when a girl was between twelve and twelve-and-a-half years old. Normally, the betrothal lasted a year, during which time the girl continued to live in her parents' home. It was only after she moved into her husband's house that the marriage was consummated; during the period of betrothal the man and the woman were not allowed to have sex.

At the time when Mary and Joseph enter upon the scene in Matthew's Gospel, Mary has been betrothed or 'engaged' to Joseph, but has yet to move into his home. Mary had probably yet to become a teenager. We are not told Joseph's age: he may well have been a teenager himself. Suddenly, to Joseph's undoubted alarm, he discovers that Mary is 'with child'. Matthew describes Mary as being 'with child from the Holy Spirit' (1:18), but at that stage this was not evident to Joseph. He must have assumed that Mary had been unfaithful to him. One thing for sure, he knew that he had nothing to do with the pregnancy: as a 'righteous man' (1:19), he observed the law. Joseph could have taken Mary to court with a view to determining whether she had been raped or whether she had consented to having sex; but he appears to have been a kind fellow, for rather than bringing public shame he decided upon a quiet divorce (1:19). Such a divorce would have involved him writing his own 'bill of divorce', which would then have had to be signed by two or three witnesses. Clearly, there was no way in which Mary's pregnancy could be kept secret, but at least it would not have been sensationalized.

It was at this point that an angel of the Lord appeared to Joseph in a dream: 'Joseph, son of David, do not be afraid to take Mary as your wife, for the child conceived in her is from the Holy Spirit' (1:20). We can but imagine the thoughts that must have gone through Joseph's head. Joseph was not naïve: he knew where babies come from, otherwise he would not have contemplated a divorce. It is probably not too much to suggest that he must have struggled with the idea of a 'virgin birth' as much as most people do today.

Actually, what was at issue was not a virgin 'birth', but a virgin 'conception'. There is no reason not to suppose that when Mary gave birth, the baby came in just the same way as all babies come, with all the accompanying pain and mess. No, Matthew (as also Luke) speak of a virginal 'conception': 'the child conceived in her is from the Holy Spirit' (1:20).

At this point sceptics have had a field day. The idea of a virginal conception, they argue, is a nonsense, if not a 'cover-up'. Mary must have had sex with someone. If not with Joseph, then with some secret lover. Alternatively, she might have been raped by a Roman soldier. Every child, rationalists argue, has to have a father and a mother.

The suggestion is frequently made that Matthew – or his source – borrowed this idea from Greek legends, which tell of gods mating with human women. But there are no parallels to the virginal conception which we find in the Gospel accounts of the birth of Jesus. For such 'divine marriages' always involve the god impregnating the woman either through normal sexual intercourse or through some substitute form of penetration. By contrast, the Spirit's work in Mary is to create new life; his role is purely creative, and not at all sexual.

There are also no parallels to virginal 'conception' in Judaism or in the Old Testament. True, Matthew cites Isaiah 7:14, but there is no evidence that this Scripture had ever before been linked with the coming of the Messiah; nor had it ever been interpreted of a virginal conception. It was only after the event that Matthew saw a special significance in this particular prophecy: there was no way in which it could have created the event. The fact is that it is difficult, if not impossible, to explain why Christians would create so many problems for themselves by promulgating such an idea, if it had no historical basis.

The historical basis of the virginal conception has, however, been put in question for some because, apart from Matthew and Luke, there is no explicit reference to virginal conception in the rest of the New Testament. The apostle Paul, for instance, appears to have no knowledge of it. Certainly, we have to acknowledge that Galatians 4:4 is no parallel: for when Paul states that in 'the fullness of time . . . God sent his Son, born of a woman, born under the law', the phrase 'born of a woman' refers to Jesus being truly man, and has as little to do with the virginal conception as has Job's description of 'A mortal, born of woman, few of days and full of trouble' (Job 14:1). However, we must take care in arguing from the silence of Scripture: for example, had there been no abuse of the Lord's Supper at Corinth, we might have assumed that Paul had no knowledge of it. The fact that Paul reflects no awareness of the virginal conception is not really different from saying that he also reflects no awareness of much else found in the Gospels.

From time to time, parallels are drawn with parthenogenesis ('virgin birth'), which is present in about one in a thousand species. Bees, frogs and worms are known to reproduce in this way. It means that eggs begin to divide and develop of their own accord, without fertilization, and eventually produce a new individual. Parthenogenesis, however, is unknown in humans. Furthermore, if Jesus had been conceived by parthenogenesis, then he would have had to be a girl, because women can only pass on X chromosomes. In normal reproductive intercourse girls are conceived when the male sperm adds a second X to the ovum's X chromosome; boys are conceived when the sperm adds a Y chromosome. Sam (R. J.) Berry, emeritus professor of genetics at University College London, has speculated that in the absence of a sperm to import a Y chromosome, Mary could have been male, but suffered a genetic mutation that had the effect of preventing target cells in her body from 'recognizing' the male sex hormone testosterone; Mary would have been chromosomally XY but would appear as a normal female. Although, as a result of androgen insensitivity, she would normally then be sterile and lack a uterus, Berry points out that the differentiation of the sex organs can be variable, and it is possible a person of this constitution could develop an ovum and a uterus. If this happened, and if the ovum developed parthenogenetically, and if a back-mutation to testosterone sensitivity took place, we would then have the situation of an apparently normal woman giving birth without intercourse to a son![2] But such rationalizing is not helpful. For what Matthew describes here is an event totally out of the ordinary, totally beyond the normal course of nature. The virginal conception is unique. The only parallels which we may draw are either the creation itself, or God's recreation evidenced in resurrection. Indeed, once we believe

---

2. R. J. Berry, 'The Virgin Birth of Christ', *Science and Christian Belief* 8 (1996), pp. 101–110.

in the God of creation and resurrection, difficulties in believing in the virginal conception disappear. True, such an argument could be seen to encourage general credulity. However, once all other options have been examined and no adequate basis found for abandoning the essential tradition of a virginal conception, then faith in the living God must step in. In this respect some words of John Taylor, a former Bishop of St Albans, are perhaps helpful:

> I find it easier to accept that when God chose to reveal himself in a human life, he did it as a one-off exercise rather than go through what the bureaucrats call 'the usual channels'. A Saviour of the world, without a touch of the miraculous at the beginning, the middle and the end of his life, I would find totally perplexing![3]

Why was Jesus 'born of a virgin'? In times past, some have argued that only in this way could Jesus be born sinless: as though the stain of original sin was transmitted through the act of conception. But this is surely a perverted view of sex. We are children, not of our parents' sin, but of their love. Others have argued that only in this way could Jesus be divine, as though divinity is linked to biology. Significantly, it was his life rather than his conception that convinced people of his divinity. Perhaps the strongest theological argument for the necessity of the virginal conception is that in this way we see that it is God alone who has done all that is necessary for salvation. The virginal conception demonstrates that we have contributed nothing to the coming of Jesus among us. Jesus is God's gift to us. Our salvation is entirely of the grace of God. Whatever the truth of these arguments, one thing is for certain: the doctrine of the virginal conception is a wonderful sign that God has come among us. Right from the start we know that Jesus is more than a man.

Joseph: a model husband and father
In Matthew's account of the birth of Jesus, Joseph is the focus of

---

3. John B. Taylor, *Preaching Through the Prophets* (Oxford: Mowbray, 1983), p. 13.

attention, and perhaps rightly so. For in many ways Joseph was the real hero of the Christmas story. He stood by his wife when most fair-minded men would have sent their wives packing. Yet, it is Mary who gets all the limelight. In most paintings of the nativity, all the emphasis is on Mary, and the baby, of course. Joseph, if he features at all, stands in the background. But Joseph was a very necessary figure, not only to the Christmas story, but to the later development of the child Jesus. Thanks to the mysterious work of the Holy Spirit, Joseph may not have been essential to the birth of Jesus: he was, however, essential to the story of Jesus.

For the preacher it takes only a little imagination to develop the picture of Joseph as a model husband and father.

In the first place, Joseph stood by his wife. Joseph must have found it incredibly difficult when Mary got pregnant. It was not surprising that he considered divorcing her. He was only doing what any other right-thinking Jewish man would have done. His parents and his friends – and no doubt, Mary's parents and her friends – would not have expected him to take any other course. But God intervened and through a dream told him to 'take Mary' (1:20) as his wife. In what must have been an extremely trying and emotionally fraught situation, Joseph had the courage and strength of character to take the dream seriously. For God's sake he was willing to go against the stream. Would that there were more Josephs today! We live in a society where divorce is regarded as almost as natural as marriage. Statistically, if you have three children, then you can reckon that at least one, if not two, of the three will end up being divorced. How different the Christian view of marriage is. In God's sight, marriage is for life. It is 'for better for worse, for richer for poorer, in sickness and in health, to love and to cherish, till death us do part'. This is not old-fashioned romanticism. This is God's plan for marriage. In the words of Jesus: 'what God has joined together, let no-one separate' (Matt. 19:6). True, there are occasions when marriages do end, when marriages irretrievably break down. Jesus too recognized that. But this is not to be the norm. One of the problems today is that many people regard the marriage covenant as a contract that can be terminated the moment one or other finds somebody else they love more. But that is a false view of marriage; it is a false view of love. We need to listen to Bonhoeffer, who, in his sermon at the wedding of his niece, said: 'It is not your love that sustains marriage, but from now on, the marriage that sustains your love.'[4] It may sound unromantic, but marriage is not about romance. It is about commitment. Thank God, many of us find romance within that commitment. But we mustn't put the cart before the horse. Husbands, be like Joseph. Be prepared to go against the stream and stand by your wives!

Secondly, Joseph proved a true father, even though he may not have sired Jesus. For had Joseph not been a good father, then almost certainly Jesus would never have taught his disciples to begin their prayer with the words 'Our Father in heaven'; let alone himself daring to call God *abba*. It was surely his own positive experience of having Joseph for a father that Jesus once told a group of fathers: 'If you . . . know how to give good gifts to your children, how much, more will your Father in heaven give good things to those who ask him!' (Matt. 7:11). The fact is that a man hasn't fulfilled his fatherly duties by causing his wife to become pregnant. Nor has he fulfilled his fatherly duties by accepting the guidelines of the Child Support Agency and paying reasonable maintenance allowance to the mother of his child. For fatherhood is about providing a child with education, stimulation, protection and security. Where there is no father, statistics show that children experience all kinds of difficulties. For instance, girls without a father in their life are two and a half times as likely to get pregnant and 53% more likely to commit suicide; boys without a father in their life are 63% more likely to run away and 37% more likely to abuse; and children without father involvement are twice as likely to abuse alcohol or drugs, twice as likely to end up in jail and four times as likely to need help for emotional or behavioural problems than those with father involvement.[5] Traditionally, we have thought of mothers as making a home for children ('homemakers'), but fathers also have a key role. Do we have time for our children, time to listen with both ears? What kind of example do we set in

4. Dietrich Bonhoeffer, quoted by Larry Christenson, *The Christian Family* (London: Fountain Trust, 1971), p. 28.

5. Judith Trowell and Alicia Etchegoyen (eds.), *A Psychoanalytical Re-evaluation of the Importance of Fathers* (Hove: Brunner-Routledge, 2002), pp. 243–244.

how we relate to our children, our wives, and indeed to people in general? What kind of picture of God will our children have because of us? Will it be for the better or the worse?

Finally, Joseph gave Jesus a religious upbringing. Like any other Jewish father, he would have taken Jesus to synagogue, as also to the temple in Jerusalem for the main religious festivals (see Luke 2:41–51). Even more importantly, Joseph would have taught Jesus about God. Whereas in our society we think of Mother as playing the major role in a child's religious development, the rabbis laid it down that one of the most important duties of fathers was instructing their children in the Law. No doubt at Passover time in Jesus' home the youngest person present would have asked: 'Why is this night different from all other nights . . . ?'; and like any other Jewish father, Joseph, beginning with Abraham, would have told the story right down to deliverance of Passover. It is not far-fetched to suggest that much of what Jesus initially learnt about God came from Joseph. So, the question arises: how do fathers match up to the example of Joseph? When I was a child we had a record at home on which an American children's choir sang: 'Don't send your kids to Sunday school: get out of bed and take them. You wouldn't want to go by yourself; don't let them feel forsaken. Some boys are good boys, some boys are bad . . . it all depends on Dad.' A little simplistic, yet it has some truth. But taking the kids to church is not enough. As the Jewish *Shema* (Deut. 6:4–7) makes clear, religious education begins at home. Practically, this may mean reading Bible stories to young children; talking through moral issues with older children; being as concerned for children's spiritual progress as for their academic progress.

The name of the Saviour

For Jews, the choice of a name for a child was an important task, for names were held to have great significance. Indeed, there was an Old Testament saying, 'as his name is, so is he' (1 Sam. 25:25). A name was held to reflect a person's character. So Abram received the new name of 'Abraham' (Gen. 17:5); and Jacob received the new name of 'Israel' (Gen. 32:28; 35:10); and at Caesarea Philippi, after Simon had confessed Jesus as 'the messiah' and 'the Son of the Living God', Jesus gave him the new name of 'Peter' (Matt. 16:17–18).

Here, in the story of Jesus' birth, Joseph is told by the angel to give his son the name of 'Jesus'. 'Jesus' is the Greek for the Hebrew 'Joshua', which was thought to be related to the Hebrew verb 'to save' and to the Hebrew noun 'salvation'. At that time, 'Jesus' was a fairly common name. For instance, in Josephus' *Antiquities*, of the twenty-eight priests who held office from the reign of Herod the Great to the fall of the temple, no fewer than four bore the name of Jesus.[6] In addition, Josephus mentions several other Jesuses, among them a general of Idumea, a priest's son, and a leader of a band of robbers. Somewhat ironically, Jesus was Barabbas' first name too (Matt. 27:16–17). But whereas Barabbas appears to have been a Jewish terrorist who sought to lead a campaign for Israel's political salvation, Jesus came to save his people 'from their sins' (1:21). Indeed, the use of a Greek pronoun (*autos*) emphasizes the fact that it is 'he', Jesus, and not anybody else, who is the Saviour.

At this stage nothing is said in the story about how Jesus will save his people from their sins. Joseph and Mary could never have dreamt that the world's salvation would involve a cross. However, when it comes to unpacking the significance of the name, preachers would be well advised to do so in the light of the rest of Matthew's Gospel. The nearest verbal parallel in Matthew is found in Jesus' words over the cup at the Last Supper: 'this is my blood of the covenant, which is poured out for many for the forgiveness of sins' (26:28). Jesus could only save his people from their sin by offering up his life for them. Only in his death could his birth receive its meaning. Another passage in Matthew's Gospel that links the theme of death with the theme of humility, which is above all exemplified in the incarnation, is found in Jesus' response to James and John: true greatness is found in the way of service: for 'the Son of Man came not to be served but to serve, and to give his life as a ransom for many' (20:28).

Nothing, either, is said about how people need to respond to Jesus' offer of salvation. The call to repent (Matt. 4:17), and by implication to believe, only comes later. However, the very manner of Jesus' coming is an indication that God does not force his salvation on anybody. Instead of being born to a couple of ordinary teenagers,

---

6. Jesus son of Phiabi, Jesus son of Sec, Jesus son of Damneus, and Jesus son of Gamaliel.

Jesus could have come in power and glory, and in so doing blinded us with his majesty. But Jesus came as a servant (see Matt. 12:18–21), and in so doing enables us to make a truly human, personal decision. God's offer of salvation in Jesus is open to all, but sadly not all respond to that invitation: the choice is ours, and on that choice depends our eternal destiny (see Matt. 22:1–14).

Nor is anything said about the new community that will be formed as a result of the salvation which Jesus brings. Yet by implication that thought is present. For although in Matthew's Gospel the term 'people' (*laos*) normally refers to Israel, Matthew is clear that the day is coming when the kingdom of God will be taken away from Israel and given to a 'people' (*ethnos*) that produces the fruits of the kingdom (Matt. 21:43). When Matthew tells that Jesus will save 'his people' from their sins, for him the phrase 'his people' therefore refers to the new people of God, the new community which is the church, made up of both Jew and Gentile, formed by the 'new covenant' God established through the blood of Jesus.

What if?

An alternative approach to this familiar text is for the preacher to speculate on names Mary and Joseph might have given to their first-born, had they been given a choice.

They might have called Jesus 'Moshe': that is, Moses. What grander name could there be for a little Hebrew boy? Moses was one of the great heroes of the Jewish people. He had led his people out of Egyptian slavery; he had led them for forty years through the wilderness. What's more, it was there in the wilderness that Moses had come down from Mount Sinai with the Ten Commandments and as a result made of Israel a true nation. A nation and its laws go hand in hand together: that's why some people are suspicious of the European Constitution, for the moment you hand over your laws, that moment you are no longer a nation. Suppose the angel had said to Joseph: 'You shall give him the name of Moses, for he will save the nation by rule of law'? But as Moses discovered in the wilderness, and many a Home Secretary in the UK has since discovered, there are limits to what even law and order can achieve. Law and order cannot make bad people good.

They might have called Jesus 'Solomon'. Now there was a king.

Why, Solomon was even greater than King David: for under Solomon, Israel reached the height of her power. But in fact, Solomon wasn't remembered for his power, but for his wisdom. It was because of his wisdom that the Queen of Sheba came to see him. It was as a result of his wisdom that the book of Proverbs came into being. What if the angel had said: 'You shall give him the name of Solomon, for he shall save the people by education'? Now, there's a thought. When Mr Blair was first elected prime minister in the UK, his theme was 'education, education, and education'. There's a lot to be said for education. We should thank God for our schools and our teachers. But education has its limits: education cannot make bad people good; education, alas, can sometimes turn people into cleverer devils.

They might have called Jesus 'Aaron'. What about Aaron for a name? Aaron, the brother of Moses, was a priest, and in his role as priest he was a pioneer of the Jewish religion. What if the angel had said: 'You shall call his name Aaron, for he shall save the people by religion'? Isn't that what people need today? Our country needs to get back to God: it needs religion. Or does it? Religion, alas, is not always a force for good. Think of the awful things done in the name of religion in Northern Ireland, let alone in the Middle East. Religion can sometimes make things worse, rather than better. Religion in itself does not make bad people good.

As it is, the angel told Joseph: 'You will name him Jesus'. At least, that's what his name is in our language. But in the language Jesus and his parents spoke it was *Yeshua*, the name translated in our English versions of the Old Testament as 'Joshua'. His name was actually *Yeshua-ben-Youssef*, Jesus son of Joseph. But why call him Jesus, *Yeshua*, Joshua? Because the name Jesus, *Yeshua*, Joshua, means 'God saves'. That is why the angel went on to say: 'You are to name him Jesus, for he will save his people from their sins.' This is what the world needs; this is what we need. Important as though law, education and religion may be, what we above all need is a Saviour, who can deal with our sin; who as a result of his cross and resurrection can actually turn bad people into good people.

Of all names in the world, Jesus is the most special name. With reason we sing the song 'Jesus, name above all names'. There is no other person who can truly bear the name of Jesus, for there is no other person who can truly save us from our sin; there is no other who can offer us forgiveness and a life that knows no end. This is why Christians found it so offensive when a company on the Continent sought to market so-called 'Jesus' jeans. Thank God the British patent office refused to allow the Luxembourg firm to register Jesus as a trademark. For as the registrar at the patent office said: 'For the majority of residents in the UK Jesus is no ordinary name. It is the name of Jesus Christ,' who we Christians declare to be the Son of God and the Saviour of the world.[7]

Emmanuel

No other section of the Gospels is so clearly linked to Old Testament prophecy as in Matthew 1 – 2. For Matthew, the birth of Jesus was very much part and parcel of the will of God. However, the theme of Jesus fulfilling the Scriptures is not limited to the opening two chapters, but runs right through the Gospel. We see this in particular in Matthew's so-called 'formula' quotations ('All this took place to fulfil what had been spoken by the Lord through the prophet'), which occur in slightly varying forms here in 1:22–23; and also in 2:15; 2:17–18; 2:23; 4:14–16; 8:17; 12:17–21; 21:4–5; 27:9–10.

Critics have sometimes alleged that the quotations shaped, if not created, the events concerned. However, the reverse is true. The quotations came later, and they simply confirm that all that happened was indeed part of God's plan for the coming Messiah. It is an interesting fact that in each case, were the quotation and formula removed, then the story would flow on without an obvious gap, which in turn suggests that they are comments added to the original stories.

Matthew's use of the prophecy found in Isaiah 7:14 is a good example of the quotation coming as an afterthought. In its original context Isaiah 7:14 has nothing to do with a virginal conception. Originally addressed by Isaiah to Ahaz, the prophecy almost certainly means that a woman who is now a virgin will by natural means, once she is united to her husband, conceive the child, Emmanuel. The Hebrew term 'almâ that is used in Isaiah 7:14 refers to a young

---

7. See *The Times*, 11 December 2003.

woman of marriageable age. Although the idea of virginity is probably implicit, it is not a technical term for a 'virgin'; whereas the
Greek term *parthenos* found in the Septuagint version of the Old
Testament does normally bear the meaning of a 'virgin'. Nonetheless,
at no stage is there any pre-Christian evidence of Isaiah 7:14 being
interpreted of a virginal conception; nor is there any evidence that
this passage was ever linked to the Messiah. It was only after the
event of Jesus' virginal conception that Christians came to link this
verse to the birth of Jesus. It may be that Matthew was also attracted
to the passage because it was this sign of 'Emmanuel' that was
addressed by Isaiah to the 'house of David' (Isa. 7:13), which Matthew
may then have seen as confirmation of the fact that Jesus was indeed
a son of David, and was not negated by the fact that Joseph was his
legal rather than his natural father.

The point of interest to the preacher, however, is not the original
meaning of the prophecy, but rather the way in which the prophecy
is applied to Jesus. Jesus is 'Emmanuel', which means 'God with us'.

There are various ways in which this thought can be unpacked. On
the one hand, it is helpful to observe the way in which Matthew in
his Gospel develops the thought of Jesus being present with his disciples. Attention is often drawn to the Great Commission at the end of
the Gospel, where the Risen Lord assures his disciples of his continued presence with them: 'I am with you always, to the end of the
age' (Matt. 28:20). However, in the context of teaching about the
church, Jesus also promises his presence: 'For where two or three are
gathered in my name, I am there among them' (Matt. 18:20). A more
uncomfortable declaration of his presence is found in the Parable of
the Sheep and the Goats, where the Lord is present in the hungry and
the thirsty, the stranger and the naked, the sick and the imprisoned
(Matt. 25:31–45).

Another approach is to reflect on the significance of the presence
of God in Jesus. If the emphasis is put on the last two words (God is
with us) then the significance of 'Emmanuel' is that God in the
person of Jesus has come to us; he has entered into the real world in
which we live; the real world where all is not 'tinsel and glitter', but
where life is so often hard and burdensome. Unfortunately, we all too
often romanticize the events surrounding the birth of Jesus and get
caught up with the shepherds and the wise men, and forget the fact

that Jesus was laid in an animal feeding trough. The manger is a telling parable of the later life of Jesus. As a young child Jesus knew what it was like to be a refugee; the fact that we hear no more of Joseph after Jesus has reached the age of twelve may well suggest that Jesus knew what it was like to live in a one-parent family; as he wandered from village to village, he knew what it was like to be a person of no fixed address, with no roof of his own under which to lie his head; he knew what it was like to experience misunderstanding and rejection; he knew what pain and suffering were all about. Precisely because Jesus has been one 'with us', Jesus knows and understands the difficulties and challenges that we may face. In the words of the writer to the Hebrews: 'we do not have a high priest who is unable to sympathize with our weaknesses' (Heb. 4:15). But then if the emphasis is put on the first word (*God* is with us), a different nuance comes to the fore. Whatever difficulties and challenges we may face, God is present. God is present with us when our world collapses around us; he is there with us even when marriages fall apart, children rebel, redundancy looms or sickness strikes. So, to quote again the writer to the Hebrews: 'Let us therefore approach the throne of grace with boldness, so that we may receive mercy and find grace to help in time of need' (Heb. 4:16).

The visit of the wise men (Matt. 2:1–12)

In the time of King Herod, after Jesus was born in Bethlehem of Judea, wise men from the East came to Jerusalem, asking, 'Where is the child who has been born king of the Jews? For we have observed his star at its rising, and have come to pay him homage.' When King Herod heard this, he was frightened, and all Jerusalem with him; and calling together all the chief priests and scribes of the people, he inquired of them where the Messiah was to be born. They told him, 'In Bethlehem of Judea; for so it has been written by the prophet:

> *"And you, Bethlehem, in the land of Judah,*
>   *are by no means least among the rulers of Judah;*
> *for from you shall come a ruler*
>   *who is to shepherd my people Israel."'*

Then Herod secretly called for the wise men and learned from them the exact time when the star had appeared. Then he sent them to Bethlehem, saying, 'Go and search diligently for the child; and when you have found him, bring me word so that I may also go and pay him homage.' When they had heard the king, they set out; and there, ahead of them, went the star that they had seen at its rising, until it stopped over the place where the child was. When they saw that the star had stopped, they were overwhelmed with joy. On entering the house, they saw the child with Mary his mother; and they knelt down and paid him homage. Then, opening their treasure-chests, they offered him gifts of gold, frankincense, and myrrh. And having been warned in a dream not to return to Herod, they left for their own country by another road.

A story rooted in history

There are people who tell us that the story of the wise men is just a story, and nothing more. Matthew, they say, simply made up the story for theological purposes. Indeed, it has been suggested that the story first came about because of such Old Testament texts as Psalm 72:10–11 and Isaiah 60:1–11. Certainly, we have to admit that many of the details as we find them in later Christian tradition are the product of imagination rather than of history.[8] However, there is no reason to doubt the essential truth of the underlying story. We can't prove that it was true, but there are a number of factors that together give it what J. B. Phillips used to call 'a ring of truth'.[9]

We know, for instance, that astrology was widely practised in the

---

8. For example, a description found in *Excerpta et Collectanea* and to be dated possibly around AD 700 states: 'The magi were the ones who gave gifts to the Lord. The first is said to have been Melchior, an old man with white hair and a long beard . . . who offered gold to the Lord as to a king. The second, Gaspar by name, young and beardless and ruddy complexioned . . . honoured him as God by his gift of incense, an oblation worthy of divinity. The third, black-skinned and heavily bearded, named Balthasar . . . by his gift of myrrh testified to the Son of Man who was to die' (quoted in R. E. Brown, *The Birth of the Messiah* [London: Geoffrey Chapman], p. 199).

9. See J. B. Phillips, *Ring of Truth: A Translator's Testimony* (London: Hodder & Stoughton, 1967).

ancient world, especially in Babylonia and Persia. It is significant that Matthew uses the term 'magi', which is a technical term for learned 'star-gazers'.

We know too that there was a widespread belief that bright new stars and conjunctions of certain constellations hailed the birth of a king. Tacitus, the Roman historian, wrote: 'The general belief is that a comet means a change of emperor', so 'when a brilliant comet now appeared . . . people speculated on Nero's successor, as though Nero were already dethroned' (*Annals* 14:22). Indeed, there is a well-attested story of the Persian king and 'magos' Tiridates, who visited Nero in AD 66 and addressed him as 'my God Mithras', and after offering homage returned to his country 'by another way'.[10] At the birth of Alexander Severus (reigned AD 222–235) a new star of great magnitude appeared in the heavens. The Christian historian Eusebius was saying nothing new when he wrote: 'In the case of remarkable and famous men we know that strange stars have appeared. What some call comets, or meteors, or tails of fire, or similar phenomena that are seen in connexion with great or unusual events.'[11]

We also know that the gifts brought by the wise men were just the kind of gifts that visitors from the east might bring. For gold, frankincense and myrrh were precious commodities that were traded between southern Arabia (now the Yemen) and the countries bordering the eastern Mediterranean. Indeed, it has been suggested that the wise men could well have stopped off at the ancient caravan city of Petra, now in southern Jordan, and bought their special gifts there.

Finally, we know that Jupiter (the 'star' of kingship) and Saturn (the 'star' of the Jews) were in conjunction three times in 7 BC. These star-gazers had good reason to make their trip.

There is then nothing inherently improbable about the story itself. So let us examine Matthew's account in greater detail.

Matthew sets the date of the wise men's visit 'in the time of King Herod' (2:1). Herod the Great reigned from 37 to 4 BC. Jesus clearly was born before 4 BC. Our present division of time into BC and AD owes its origin to Dionysius the Small who in AD 525 was asked by

---

10. Dio Cassius 63.1–7; Pliny, *Naturalis historia* 30.16–17; Suetonius, *Nero* 13.

11. Eusebius, *Demonstratio evangelica* 9.1.

Pope John I to prepare a standard calendar for the Western Church that would be reckoned from the date of Jesus' birth. Unfortunately, Dionysius miscalculated the birth of Jesus, and so we have the anomaly that Jesus was born several years BC!

Even if we knew the precise date of Jesus' birth, we still would not know when the wise men visited him. For, the fact that in Christian tradition the feast of Epiphany falls twelve days after Christmas Day does not mean that the wise men actually arrived twelve days after the birth of Jesus. It was probably a good deal later. Indeed, the fact that Herod later gave orders to kill all the boys in and around Bethlehem who were two years old or younger (2:16) indicates that probably at least a year had passed.

Furthermore, we are not to imagine Mary and Joseph still living in temporary accommodation. The impression we receive from Matthew 2:11 is that Mary and Joseph were already living in their own house, or if not their own house, then in rented property.

Matthew uses the term 'magi' to describe the wise men. Originally, this term referred to a priestly caste of the Medes and Persians who specialized in interpreting dreams, but later it was used to describe men of particular intellectual ability, including astrologers. The Hawaiian pidgin version of the New Testament calls the 'magi' 'Da Smart Guys who know plenny bout da stars'! These wise men may have come from Persia; on the other hand, they may well have come from Babylon or from Arabia. Matthew simply tells us that they came 'from the East' (2:1).

The tradition that these wise men were three kings has no foundation in history. The number three arose simply because of the three gifts that they presented. The idea that they were kings appears to have arisen from reflection on such passages as Psalm 72:10–11 and Isaiah 60:1–11, which speak of kings bringing gifts to God's king and falling down before him.

The exact nature of the star that the wise men saw has been a matter of much speculation. One long-favoured suggestion is that the wise men saw a comet. Comets move in regular but elliptical paths around the sun. When they come close to the sun and to the earth, they can be striking, especially if they develop a luminous tail of gasses and dust. Remarkably, bright comets appear only a few times each century. We know that Halley's comet (named after Edmund

Halley, an eighteenth-century astronomer), which appears every seventy-six years, made an appearance in 12–11 BC. Unfortunately, such a date would be a very long time before the birth of Jesus, which is usually dated around 6 BC. An alternative suggestion is the wise men saw a 'supernova' or 'new star'. A supernova involves a faint or very distant star in which an explosion takes place, so that for a few weeks or months it gives out so much light that it can even be visible in daytime. About a dozen such stars are discovered each year, but the ones visible to the naked eye are much rarer. Unfortunately, there is no record of such a star appearing around the birth of Jesus. The present scholarly consensus appears to be that it was a conjunction of the planets. In the course of their orbits Jupiter and Saturn pass each other every twenty years. A much rarer occurrence, which happens every 805 years, is when Mars passes during or shortly after the conjunction of Jupiter and Saturn, so that the three planets are close together. From calculations, we know that unusually there were three high points in 7 BC when Jupiter and Saturn were in conjunction, and that Mars passed early the next year. Since Jupiter was deemed be the 'royal' planet, and since Saturn was sometimes thought to represent the Jews, the wise men might well have had reason to conclude that a new king of the Jews was born. This conclusion would have fitted in with an expectation which was around at that time, and which was recorded both by Suetonius and Tacitus, that a world-ruler was to come from Judea.[12]

The arrival of the wise men in Judea must have caused consternation to Herod and his court. As an Edomite and a Roman nominee, he would have viewed any messianic royal pretender with claims to the throne of David as a real threat. An insecure man, he was ruthless in the suppression of those he perceived to be his rivals.

In response to Herod's enquiry as to 'where the Messiah was to be born' (2:4), the religious leaders pointed to Bethlehem on the basis of Micah 5:2. Matthew reproduces a somewhat free version of Micah: for instance, the ancient name of Bethlehem, 'Ephrathah', is replaced by the currently more recognizable term of 'in the land of Judah'. Furthermore, Micah's statement of Bethlehem's insignificance is

---

12. Suetonius, *Vespasianus* 4; Tacitus, *Annals* 5.13.

reversed by the addition of 'by no means'. Matthew also conflates the Micah text with words drawn from 2 Samuel 5:2, where David is described as 'the shepherd of . . . Israel'.

So the wise men set off following the star to Bethlehem. It may seem strange that Herod did not send some of his troops to accompany them, but presumably the sight of soldiers at that stage might have jeopardized the search for the child. It is also perhaps a little strange that none of the religious leaders went with them; one might have thought they had an interest in the fulfilment of Scripture!

Precisely how the star actually led them to the house where Jesus was is something of a mystery. Stars do not normally stop off at a particular house! However, in one early Christian tradition the star went and stood over the head of Jesus (*Protevangelium of James* 21.3)!

The 'joy' of the wise men (Matt. 2:10) is understandable. At last, after days and months of searching, they had found the object of their search. No wonder they were 'overwhelmed' with joy. In Luke's Gospel the angel announces 'good news of great joy' (Luke 2:10). Joy, along with a sense of awe, is a proper response to the Christmas story.

On entering the house they 'paid homage' (Matt. 2:11) to the newborn king. The Greek text suggests that they did not simply kneel down, but actually prostrated themselves, falling down on their faces before him. Within Judaism such prostration would have been proper only to the worship of God.

The wise men brought expensive gifts. In the Bible gold has a long history of being a precious metal, and was eminently suitable as a gift fit for a king. Frankincense was a sweet-smelling gum resin that came from various trees and bushes. According to Exodus 30:34–38, it was an ingredient of the incense offered before the Lord; while according to Leviticus, it was to be offered with the Bread of the Presence (see Lev. 24:7) and added to cereal offerings (Lev. 2:1–2, 14–16; 6:14–16). Myrrh was also a fragrant gum resin and was used for a variety of perfumes (see Esth. 2:12; Ps. 45:8). The use of myrrh in the crucifixion (Mark 15:23) and burial (John 19:39) has led to the tradition that it symbolizes suffering and death, but in the Old Testament it was a symbol of joy and festivity (Ps. 45:8; Prov. 7:17; Song 3:6; 5:5). Perhaps significantly, Matthew in his account of the crucifixion has removed the reference to myrrh (27:34).

Wise men came asking

Matthew tells us: 'wise men . . . came . . . asking' (Matt. 2:1–2). Yes, it is precisely the wise who are not afraid to ask questions. It is only the stupid whose minds are so made up that they are not prepared to question the evidence for themselves. The wise men who searched for Jesus were skilled in philosophy, medicine and natural science: they were the intellectuals of their day. They came because their curiosity had been aroused by a special star.

Today, if we would be wise, we too need to ask questions. But in the first instance we need to ask not 'Where is the baby born to be the king of the Jews?', but 'Who is this baby born to be the king of the Jews?' To answer that question we do not need to search the heavens as did those wise men: we need to 'search' (AV) or 'examine' the Scriptures (see Acts 17:11). We need to examine the evidence to find out who this Jesus is. Yes, if we would be wise, we need to read the Gospels; to read not simply their account of the birth of Jesus, but also their account of the life, death and resurrection of Jesus. The wise will not be satisfied with impressions gained as a child; rather, they will come to the Gospel story with adult minds and will ask adult questions. I guarantee that wise people with open minds will discover that there is no other way for accounting for Jesus than finding him to be the Son of God and the Saviour of the world.

Sadly, too many have made up their minds without examining the evidence. In this respect the New Testament translator J. B. Phillips wrote:

> Over the years I have had hundreds of conversations with people, many of them of higher intellectual calibre than my own, who quite obviously had no idea of what Christianity is really about. I was in no case trying to catch them out; I was simply and gently trying to find out what they knew about the New Testament. My conclusion was that they knew virtually nothing. This I find pathetic and somewhat horrifying. It means that the most important Event in human history is politely and quietly by-passed. For it is not as though the evidence had been examined and found unconvincing; it had simply never been examined.[13]

13. Phillips, *Ring of Truth*, p. 11.

'Wise men . . . came . . . asking'. We too need to be wise and to ask questions. We too need to examine the evidence, whether it be in reading the Gospels or attending an Alpha course. Peter Abelard, the French philosopher and theologian, was right when he said: 'The first key to wisdom is assiduous and frequent questioning. For by doubting we come in inquiry and by inquiry we arrive at truth.'[14] It is only by asking that we discover the truth as it is in Jesus.

The challenge of the star

The star is a challenge to adventure. In a very real sense the wise men – whether they were three or, as one tradition has it, twelve in number – were adventurers. They were adventurers in the sense that they left their homes to find Jesus, the newborn king. In the course of that great adventure they covered hundreds of miles: hundreds of miles in a world where there was no motorway network, where there were no intercity trains or jumbo jets to take. Travel by camel was surely arduous. And yet they came looking for Jesus. In many ways it was an adventure of faith. When they left home, their destination was unknown. They had no precise forwarding address. They simply followed a star. The parallels with the Christian faith are surely clear. For Jesus calls us too on an adventure. Indeed, according to Sir Wilfred Grenfell, a distinguished Christian missionary doctor and Labrador explorer of a former generation: 'The Christian life is the only real adventure.'

The star is also a challenge to thought. The 'magi' were wise men who studied the starts. The conjunction of Saturn and Jupiter or whatever it was, caused them to ponder and to think. Their decision to follow the star was not based on a whim, but no doubt involved all sorts of calculations. So too today the star challenges us to think about the claims of the Christian faith. For the Christian faith does require thought and reflection. In this respect the humanist group were mistaken, who at the time of a university Christian mission circulated posters saying, 'Join the Christian Union now. Entrance fee: your critical faculty and personal independence.' The Christian faith

---

14. M. H. Manser (ed.), *The Westminster Collection of Christian Quotations* (Louisville: Westminister/John Knox Press, 2001), p. 399.

has always attracted many of the great thinkers of the day. It is true that thought alone is not sufficient: faith too comes into play. But it is not the kind of faith that flies in the face of all human reason. In the words of Pope John Paul II's 1998 encyclical letter *Fides et Ratio* (Faith and Reason):

> Faith and reason are like two wings on which the human spirit rises to the contemplation of truth; and God has placed in the human heart a desire to know the truth – in a word to know himself – so that, by knowing and loving God, men and women may also come to the fullness of truth about themselves.[15]

Just as the journey of the magi involved a combination of thought and faith, so too does the journey of faith today.

The star too is a challenge to us all. Nobody really knows from where the wise men came. In early Christian art the wise men were always depicted in Persian dress: wearing belted tunics with sleeves, trousers and Persian caps. This depiction led to a famous incident in AD 614, when the Persian army swept over Palestine, wreaking havoc and setting churches to the torch. When they came to Bethlehem, however, they spared the church, because of a mosaic picturing the magi as Persians; they recognized their fellow countrymen. Others, however, have speculated that the wise men came from Babylon. We know that the Babylonians developed a great interest in astronomy and astrology. Moreover, although in the sixth century BC many Jews returned to Jerusalem when the Exile came to end, a large colony of Jews remained in Babylon, and so it is possible that the Babylonian astrologers could have learned something of Jewish messianic expectations. Yet others have speculated that they came from Arabia, or even from Africa. We don't know. But, there is a positive side to our ignorance. The very fact that we don't know means that these wise men can the more easily be representative of us all. The star doesn't just challenge people from the East; it challenges us all to go to Bethlehem and bring to the Christ our gifts.

---

15. See further, Alister E. McGrath, *Theology: The Basics* (Oxford: Blackwell, 2004), pp. 7–9.

A limited star

The star in itself was insufficient. Had the wise men only the star to follow, they would probably never have found Jesus. This does not mean to say that the star had no role to play. For had there been no star, they would never have set out on their long journey; they would never have begun their quest to find Jesus. And yet, the star by itself was insufficient. It led them only to Herod. True, it later led them to the place where Jesus was (Matt. 2:9), but nonetheless it lacked precision. Something more was needed. That something more is the Scriptures. We see this when Herod asked his own wise men, the priest and the scribes, where the Messiah was to be born: they pointed to Micah 5 and perhaps to 2 Samuel 2. The Scriptures played a crucial role in their search. The significance for us is surely obvious.

Today wise people still seek Jesus; they seek Jesus because they realize from the evidence of the created order that there is more to life than first meets the eye. As Paul put it: 'Ever since the creation of the world his eternal power and divine nature, invisible though they are, have been understood and seen through the things he has made' (Rom. 1:20). The very structure and design of the world in which we live is an indication to the wise that this is not just our world; it is God's world. In the words of the German philosopher Immanuel Kant: 'Two things fill the mind with ever new and increasing wonder and awe, the more often and the more seriously reflection concentrates upon them: the starry heaven above me and the moral law within me.'[16] So natural theology has a place, but a study of the universe in itself is insufficient to bring anybody to Jesus.

If we would find Jesus, we must turn to the Scriptures. There may be other things that in the first place arouse our attention: it might be the fact of the created order, or it might be the loving witness of a friends. But only the Scriptures themselves lead us to Jesus – for only they reveal who he was and what he came to do. As Paul wrote to Timothy: the Scriptures 'are able to instruct you for salvation through faith in Christ Jesus' (2 Tim. 3:15). Or, as John put it, he wrote his Gospel 'that you may come to believe that Jesus is the Messiah, the Son of God, and that through believing you may have life in his

---

16. Immanuel Kant, *Critique of Practical Reason* (1788), 2.

name' (John 20:31). This is why we continue to read and preach from
the Scriptures. The Scriptures are an essential part of our witness: for
only by their means may Jesus be found.

A missionary story

The story of the wise men is a missionary story. In one sense, this is
not really a story about wise men at all. It so happened that they
were wise men, but it would have made no odds if they had been
shepherds or tinkers, tailors, soldiers or sailors. Their profession is
irrelevant. What interested Matthew was that these wise men came
'from the East' (2:1)! Where precisely the East was, we don't know.
Nor does it matter. The crucial point is that they came beyond Israel.
These men were Gentiles. This is a story of Gentiles acknowledging
Jesus as King.

It may well be that Matthew is actually making a contrast between
Herod and all of Jerusalem, on the one hand, and the wise men on
the other. For while the Saviour was rejected by his own people, he
was welcomed by the wider non-Jewish world. This is a point worth
underlining. We often speak of Matthew's Gospel as being the most
Jewish of Gospels, and in many ways it is. Matthew, for instance,
spoke not of the 'kingdom of God' but of the 'kingdom of heaven';
for like any good Jew he found it difficult to use the name of God,
and so if at all possible he tried to find a circumlocution. Yet Matthew
is as clear as any that the Christian Gospel broke through all barriers,
nationalistic or otherwise. Jesus may have been the 'Son of David',
but – as he showed through the genealogy of Jesus – he was also the
'Son of Abraham' (1:1), Abraham by whom the descendants of all the
nations would bless themselves (see Gen. 22:18). The visit of the wise
men to see the baby Jesus may be viewed as an anticipation of the
promise of Jesus that we find in Matthew 8:11: 'many will come from
east and west and will eat with Abraham and Isaac and Jacob in the
kingdom of heaven'. As Matthew's Gospel begins with the adoration
of the magi, so it ends with the Great Commission, where Jesus commands his followers to 'Go . . . and make disciples of all nations'
(Matt. 28:19).

In this respect the story of the wise men fulfils the prophecies of
Psalm 72 and Isaiah 60. For in Psalm 72 we read of his kingdom reach-
ing 'from sea to sea', from the river Euphrates to the ends of the earth.

May the kings of Tarshish [Spain] and of the isles
   render him tribute,
may the kings of Sheba and Seba bring gifts.
May all kings fall down before him,
   all nations give him service. (Ps. 72:10–11)

Although it may well be from this passage that the wise men were identified as kings, the point here is not so much that kings will come, but that nations will come and serve him. A similar emphasis is found in Isaiah 60 where Isaiah exhorts Jerusalem to:

Arise, shine; for your light has come
   and the glory of the LORD has risen upon you.

Nations shall come your light,
   and kings to the brightness of your dawn.

   the wealth of the nations shall come to you.
A multitude of camels shall cover you,
   the young camels of Midian and Ephah;
   all those from Sheba shall come.
They shall bring gold and frankincense,
   and shall proclaim the praise of the LORD. (Isa. 60:1, 3, 5b–6)

Again the point at issue is that the nations will be drawn to the light brought about by the coming of the Messiah; the fact that kings too will come is incidental.

Matthew, through including this story in his Gospel, is pointing to the fact that Jesus is the Saviour of the world. Clearly, this has implications for us, for it means that Jesus is our Saviour too. Indeed, he is not just our Saviour, he is also our neighbour's Saviour. To celebrate the coming of the wise men is to recognize that we have a task to make the Saviour known. We are called to a missionary enterprise, a missionary enterprise that first and foremost is not about taking the good news of Jesus to far-off lands (for many of them know far more about Jesus than we do), but about taking the good news of Jesus to people who live and work here in our neighbourhood.

Hope fulfilled

Has it ever struck us is how strange it was that these wise men from the East should have sought a Jewish king? For when they came to Herod, they asked: 'Where is the child who has been born king of the Jews? For we observed his star at its rising, and have come to pay him homage' (Matt. 2:2). Why on earth should they worship the king of the Jews? They were not his subjects! They came from elsewhere. What possible relevance could this baby hold for them? I believe that they realized, however dimly, that this Jewish baby was the one who was going to fulfil all their hopes, as indeed the hopes of the world. He it was who was going to bring an end to all the suffering and strife the world had known, and establish a kingdom of peace.

At that time there was a widespread expectation that looked for a world ruler who would bring peace to the world. The great Roman poet Virgil, writing in 40 BC, composed his so-called *Fourth Eclogue*, in which he mentions his hope of a virgin and a divinely descended child, before whom all the earth will tremble in homage, when the 'remaining traces of guilt' would disappear and a new age of peace would be established, in which fear would be no more. He dreamt of an age of gold, when, he said, 'without being called, the goats will come home, their udders swollen with milk; and the herds will not be afraid of the mighty lions . . . the plain will slowly become golden with waving grain, and the ripening grape will hang from the wild briars, and the stern oaks will yield dewy drops of honey.'[17] Significantly, Zoroastrianism, the religion of Persia, taught of a saviour-king who would come from the West and bring in the kingdom of God. So when the wise men came to worship the baby Jesus, they worshipped him not just as the king of the Jews, but as the *king of the world*.

I find it significant that the only other place in the Gospels where the expression 'king of the Jews' is found occurs in the story of the crucifixion. The Gospel writers tell us that Pilate put over the head of Jesus an inscription 'The king of the Jews', written in the three main languages of the ancient world: Greek, Latin and Hebrew. Whether

---

17. See further, R. E. Brown, *The Birth of the Messiah* (London: Geoffrey Chapman, 1977), p. 566.

or not he intended it, Pilate was in effect saying, 'Jesus is not just the king of the Jews; he is the world's king.'

And that is certainly the claim of Christians. We know from our experience that Jesus fulfils not simply the hopes of the Jews for a Messiah; he fulfils the hopes of us all for a new beginning and a new life. What's more, the day is coming when he will bring in his kingdom of peace, and on that day

> people shall beat their swords into ploughshares,
>> and their spears into pruning-hooks;
> nation shall not lift up sword against nation,
>> neither shall they learn war any more. (Mic. 4:3)

Or in the words of Isaiah:

> a child has been born for us,
>> a son given to us;
> authority rests upon his shoulders;
>> and he is named . . .
> Prince of Peace. (Isa. 9:6)

Here is a message of hope for our suffering, war-torn world. The Herods of this world may do their worst, but their time is limited. The day will come when every knee will bow and every tongue will confess that Jesus Christ is Lord.

Costly worship

When the wise men worshipped Jesus, 'they offered him gifts of gold, frankincense, and myrrh' (Matt. 2:11b). In time these gifts were interpreted symbolically: gold for a king, frankincense for a god, and myrrh for one who was going to die. However, the twelfth-century monk Bernard of Clairvaux offered a more practical interpretation, suggesting that the gold was to assist the holy family with their trip to Egypt; the frankincense, to sweeten the air in the stable; and the myrrh, to get rid of worms from Christ's intestines![18]

---

18. Gabriele Finaldi, *The Image of Christ* (London: National Gallery, 2000), p. 66.

The truth is that we should probably not differentiate between the various gifts: the gifts they offered were all gifts for a king. They offered Jesus their best: their best, which happened to be gold, frankincense and myrrh.

Our worship too should express itself in giving. And in giving to Jesus we too should give our best. With David we should say: 'I will not offer . . . offerings to the LORD my God that cost me nothing' (2 Sam. 24:24). For worship that costs nothing is precisely that: nothing!

What have we to bring to Jesus? In the first place, we have ourselves to bring. So in his letter to the Romans, after having spent much time reflecting on what God has done for us in Jesus, the apostle Paul went on: 'I appeal to you therefore, brothers and sisters, by the mercies of God, to present your bodies as a living sacrifice, holy and acceptable to God, which is your spiritual worship' (Rom. 12:1). God has a claim upon all that we are and have. In our worship we are called to give of ourselves totally and unreservedly. Such worship is indeed costly. But as C. T. Studd used to say: 'If Jesus Christ be God and died for me, then no sacrifice can be too great.'

One consequence that arises from the giving of ourselves to God is the giving of our money. As the writer to the Hebrews put it, we are to share what we have, 'for such sacrifices are pleasing to God' (Heb. 13:16). William Temple, a former Archbishop of Canterbury, once called Christianity the most materialistic of all religions, since the practical outworking of it touches every area of our daily life, including our pockets. Here too is a message for each one of us. If Jesus is indeed the Saviour of the World and the Lord of all, then he deserves our all. David Watson, the Anglican evangelist, used to tell the story of a woman who once asked her husband: 'Can you give me a little money?' Watson commented: ' "How little?" That is so often the attitude of Christians today. How little can I give with a clear conscience.' He went on to ask, 'If our wages or salary were ten times the amount we give to God each week, would we be well off?'[19]

---

19. David Watson, *I Believe in the Church* (London: Hodder & Stoughton, 1978), p. 189.

The Scriptures too exhort us to come with our praises: 'Through him, then, let us continually offer a sacrifice of praise to God, that is, the fruit of lips that confess his name' (Heb. 13:15). Worship, if it is for real, must always be God-centred. When we come to worship God, we come to give God our praise. Alas, sometimes we get our priorities wrong: when we go to church, we go perhaps to get rather than to give. In this respect I am reminded of a notice-board that stood outside a church and read: 'Join us for worship. You will feel better for it!' That may be true, but that is not the purpose of worship. Worship involves giving. What's more, worship involves cost. In a day when many Christians tend to go to church twice a month, it may take self-discipline to make worship a priority. When the weather is inclement, it may take an effort to brave the elements to go to worship. When friends we haven't seen for a while drop in for a visit, it may take courage to put God first. But true worship always involves cost.

The wise men offered costly gifts to Jesus, and so too should we!

The gift of myrrh

The story is told of a group of children who put on a nativity play for their parents. The first three came in; one played the part of Mary, another the part of Joseph, while the third played the part of an angel. Then the last child came in riding a camel. At least, she moved as though she were riding a camel, because she had on her mother's high-heeled shoes. She was bedecked in all the jewellery available and carried a pillow laden with certain items. She bowed before Mary and Joseph and announced: 'I am all three Wise Men. I bring precious gifts: gold, circumstance and mud.' Yes, children find it difficult to cope with the gifts the wise men brought: 'gold, frankincense and myrrh'. Indeed, if we are honest, some of us too get confused.

Gold we all know; many of us wear wedding rings made of gold. Frankincense is known to us too, albeit to a lesser degree, but most of us have had the experience of burning joss sticks. But myrrh. What exactly was it? According to the *New Bible Dictionary*, myrrh is 'the resinous exudate from incisions on the stems and branches of a low shrubby tree, either the *Commiphora myrrha* or the closely related *Commiphora kataf*. Both species are native to Arabia and adjacent parts of Africa. The gum oozes from the wounds as "tears" which harden to form an oily yellowish-brown resin'.[20]

Why did the wise men offer the baby Jesus myrrh? Matthew makes it clear that it was their way of honouring Jesus as King of the Jews. Indeed, before presenting their treasures, Matthew tells us that 'they knelt down and paid homage' to the baby Jesus. Paying homage, offering gifts, it was all one and the same thing. They presented to Jesus expensive gifts fit for a king. We see this in 1 Kings 10:1–2, where we read that 'When the queen of Sheba heard of the fame of Solomon' she 'came to Jerusalem with a very great retinue, with camels bearing spices, and very much gold, and precious stones'. The spices may well have included myrrh. In Isaiah 60:6 we read of camels coming from the east bringing 'gold and frankincense'; these were gifts to honour Israel's God. Psalm 45:7–8 tells of a king being anointed with myrrh: 'God, your God, has anointed you . . . your robes are all fragrant with myrrh and aloes and cassia'.

Yet there is something to be said for the tradition that sees myrrh as a gift fit for the king who came to die. In the words of the third king in John Henry Hopkins's well-known carol 'We three kings':

> Myrrh is mine, its bitter perfume
> Breathes a life of gathering gloom;
> Sorrowing, sighing, bleeding, dying,
> Sealed in a stone-cold tomb.

The gift of myrrh reminds us that the babe of Bethlehem came to be the Christ of Calvary. His death was no accident, nor did it betoken a change of plan. As Jesus himself said to his disciples: 'the Son of Man came . . . to give his life a ransom for many' (Matt. 20:28). The cross cannot be separated from the cradle. Jesus came to die. The artist Holman Hunt captured this truth in a picture of Jesus at the door of his father's shop. Jesus is still only a boy. The setting sun is shining at the door, and Jesus has come to the door to stretch his limbs, which had grown cramped over the bench. He stands there in the doorway

---

20. J. D. Douglas et al. (eds.), *New Bible Dictionary* (Leicester: IVP, 3rd ed., 1996), p. 466.

with his arms outstretched, and behind him, on the wall, the setting sun throws his shadow: the shadow of a cross.[21] In the background is Mary. As she sees that shadow there is the fear of the coming tragedy in her eyes. Similarly, T. S. Eliot in his poem 'Journey of the Magi' has the visitors from the East see, on their way to Bethlehem, 'three trees on the low sky' and 'six hands at an open door dicing for pieces of silver'. The three trees stand for the three crosses, while the men dicing for silver represent the soldiers casting lots for Jesus' garments and Judas' betrayal of his master for thirty pieces of silver.[22]

Christmas is rightly a time for joy and festivity. But it is also a time for solemn reflection. For Christmas is not an end in itself; rather, Christmas marks the beginning of a path that led to a cross. A sign of this was the gift of myrrh.

The aftermath of the wise men's visit (Matt. 2:13–23)

Now after they had left, an angel of the Lord appeared to Joseph in a dream and said, 'Get up, take the child and his mother, and flee to Egypt, and

---

21. Many earlier painters had also sought to link the nativity with the crucifixion. For example, Giovanni Bellini's *The Madonna of the Meadow* (c. 1500) depicts the child Jesus asleep on Mary's lap, which for devout viewers would inevitably have recalled the *Pieta*, where the dead Christ lies across Mary's lap. In Bellini's picture Jesus' hand, placed across his chest, recalls the pose traditionally adopted for burial, while the rigidity of his right leg evokes the stiffness of death. In Murillo's *The Christ Child Resting on the Cross* (c. 1670s) Jesus is depicted as innocently resting on a cross of size and proportions appropriate to his small stature; beside him is a skull. For further illustrations see Finaldi, *The Image of Christ*, pp. 44–73.

22. W. D. Davies and Dale C. Allison, *The Gospel according to Saint Matthew*, I, International Critical Commentary (Edinburgh: T. & T. Clark, 2nd ed., 2000), p. 254, comment: 'Matthew would have approved of Eliot's interpretation. We have had occasion to observe several connexions between Mt 2 and the passion narrative, such as the gathering of the Jewish leaders, the title, "king of the Jews", and the decision of the ruling authority to do away with Jesus. Matthew wants the end foreshadowed in the beginning.'

remain there until I tell you; for Herod is about to search for the child, to destroy him.' Then Joseph got up, took the child and his mother by night, and went to Egypt, and remained there until the death of Herod. This was to fulfil what had been spoken by the Lord through the prophet, 'Out of Egypt I have called my son.'

When Herod saw that he had been tricked by the wise men, he was infuriated, and he sent and killed all the children in and around Bethlehem who were two years old or under, according to the time that he had learned from the wise men. Then was fulfilled what had been spoken through the prophet Jeremiah:

> *'A voice was heard in Ramah,*
> *wailing and loud lamentation,*
> *Rachel weeping for her children;*
> *she refused to be consoled, because*
> *they are no more.'*

When Herod died, an angel of the Lord suddenly appeared in a dream to Joseph in Egypt and said, 'Get up, take the child and his mother, and go to the land of Israel, for those who were seeking the child's life are dead.' Then Joseph got up, took the child and his mother, and went to the land of Israel. But when he heard that Archelaus was ruling over Judea in the place of his father Herod, he was afraid to go there. And after being warned in a dream, he went away to the district of Galilee. There he made his home in a town called Nazareth, so that what had been spoken through the prophets might be fulfilled, 'He will be called a Nazorean.'

The threat to Jesus

Many commentators do not believe the story of the escape to Egypt or indeed the later story of the massacre of the children. They write them off as imaginative creations of Matthew, who, they allege, was simply elaborating on his theme of Jesus fulfilling the Old Testament Scriptures. However, as we have already seen before, the Old Testament prophecies to which Matthew refers are his way of reflecting theologically on the past; they do not create the event themselves. It is true that Luke has no knowledge of these two incidents; but all this means is that Matthew was simply drawing upon a different source for his information.

Again, an angel speaks to Joseph in a dream, but this time to warn him of impending disaster (2:13). The choice of Egypt as a haven of refuge was a natural one. Apart from anything else, it was outside Herod's jurisdiction. We have no idea of where in Egypt Joseph and Mary together with Jesus fled to. They may simply have gone a few miles over the border. Or they may have gone as far as Alexandria, where the Jews formed two-fifths of the population. Imaginative Coptic legends, however, have Jesus sailing hundreds of miles down the Nile. Matthew sees the escape into Egypt as a fulfilment of Scripture (2:15). Matthew's choice of Scripture is somewhat strange, in so far as Hosea 11:1 does not refer to an individual, but to Israel; furthermore, it was not a prophecy, but rather an account of Israel's origin. However, the general truth remains: Israel's experience prefigured Jesus' experience.

Joseph and his family remained in Egypt until the death of Herod in 4 BC, when his kingdom was divided between his sons. Archelaus, who took over Idumea, Judah and Samaria, got off to a bad start: before he left for Rome to contest his father's will, he overreacted to some trouble that occurred at Passover time and as a result killed about three thousand pilgrims. Understandably, Joseph did not want to return to Bethlehem. Instead, Joseph took his family back to Nazareth, where Archelaus' half-brother, Herod Antipas, was king. Again, Matthew sees this move as a fulfilment of Scripture, although which particular Scripture Matthew had in mind is uncertain: Isaiah 11:1, where the Messiah is described as a 'branch' (Hebrew: nēṣer) from the root of Jesse, is one possibility; and Judges 13:5, where Samson is presented as a Nazirite (Greek: naziraios) is another.

Our interest centres primarily on the so-called 'massacre of the innocents' (2:16–18). Although there is no independent verification of this event, this dreadful act is totally in line with the kind of person Herod became. For after a relatively good beginning, he degenerated into a butcher of a man. For instance, he killed his wife Mariamne, and his two sons Alexander and Aristobulus. This caused Emperor Augustus to observe cynically that it was better to be Herod's pig than his son! To ensure that there was mourning at his funeral, Herod ordered his soldiers to kill notable political prisoners: 'So shall all Judea and every household weep for me, whether they wish it or not.'[23] Herod was an insecure man, fearful of any kingly rival or messianic pretender. It was not surprising then that he was deeply disturbed when he heard of the birth of a baby in Bethlehem, for whom the magi claimed the title king. Unable to trick them into disclosing the child's identity, he sent in his troops to butcher every male child under the age of two. True, it did not involve hundreds of children, for Bethlehem was not a large town. Bearing in mind the high mortality rate of that time, it has been estimated that, if Bethlehem had a population of around one thousand, then almost certainly no more than twenty boys at the most would have been killed. Not that this makes the crime any less black.

At last Herod's appalling mission was completed and the troops left. Only one sound filled the air: the sound, says Matthew, that Jeremiah had heard centuries before: 'A voice was heard in Ramah, wailing and loud lamentation. Rachel weeping for her children; she refused to be consoled, because they are no more' (Matt. 2:17–18).

Originally, these words from Jeremiah 31:15 had no connection with Herod's slaughter of the children; they were written hundreds of years before the event. Jeremiah first penned these words to depict the people of Jerusalem being led away in exile. On their sad way the exiles passed Rachel's tomb in Ramah, a town just the other side of Jerusalem from Bethlehem. Jeremiah pictures Rachel weeping, even in her tomb, for the fate that had befallen the people.

Jesus came to a world of pain and sorrow
For the preacher this story is a pointer to the fact that Jesus came into our world of pain and sorrow. Jesus was born in no Garden of Eden: not for him a life of sunshine, free of tears. No, Jesus was born in Bethlehem, a town associated with pain, sorrow and death. We need to be reminded of this. All too often the Bethlehem at the centre of our Christmas festivities is remote from the harsh realities of the world in which we live. For us Bethlehem has become a town associated with romance, dream and sentiment. On Christmas Eve we often sing Phillips Brooks's hymn

---

23. Josephus, *War* 1.33.6; *Antiquities* 17.6.5.

O little town of Bethlehem,
  How still we see you lie!
Above your deep and dreamless sleep
  The silent stars go by.

From the quietness of Christmas Eve we move on to the jollity of Christmas Day, when we may well sing Valerie Collinson's modern song 'Come and join the celebration'.

Bethlehem is then a place of light and of joy. And when we are not in church, Bethlehem is associated with an excuse for a merry round of Christmas parties and festivities. It becomes an escape from the real world where life is tough and the innocent all too often suffer. How different was the reality. And what a difference that reality makes. The fact is that life for many is tough. There have been times when we have wept, when we have been hurt, when we have experienced loss or sorrow of one kind or another. What a comfort it is to know that Jesus understands, for the babe of Bethlehem is also the Man of Sorrows.

But, thank God, there is more to celebrate than just that Jesus came into our world of pain and sorrow. Jesus also came to deal with our pain and our sorrow. The fact is that the cries of Rachel are but passing. Our tears will one day turn to laughter. It is not without significance that the verse which Matthew quotes from Jeremiah 31 to describe the weeping of Rachel is the only gloomy verse in the chapter. As a whole, Jeremiah 31 is a chapter vibrant with hope. For instance,

they shall be radiant over the goodness of the LORD . . .

Then shall the young women rejoice in the dance,
  and the young men and the old shall be merry.
I will turn their mourning into joy,
  I will comfort them, and give them gladness for sorrow.

there is hope for your future, says the LORD:
  your children shall come back to
    their own country. (31:12b, 13, 17)

Jeremiah goes on to speak of a 'new covenant' God is going to make with his people; he will be their God, they will be his people (31:31–34). The good news is that in Jesus God has made a new covenant. For through the world-shattering events of the cross and resurrection Jesus has dealt with sin, that potent force which is at the root of all the world's injustice and suffering. There on the cross and in his resurrection Jesus has set in motion a process that one day will be completed in a new world where 'Death will be no more; mourning and crying and pain will be no more' (Rev. 21:4). Jesus is in the business of making all things new. At this moment his work is not complete. God has dealt the decisive blow to sin and death, but there is still potency in their death throes. If you like, D-Day is behind us, but VE Day has yet to come. We live in the in-between times, between the coming of Jesus in humility and his coming in glory. But in these in-between times Jesus offers us his Spirit, who encourages us when we are downhearted, who brings comfort to us in our sorrow, who draws alongside us in our pain, and who strengthens us in our weakness. Yes, we have much to celebrate.

Herod died; the child lived

It is a historical fact that after a reign of some thirty-three or so years marked by violence and intrigue, Herod the Great died a lonely and horrible death of cancer at Jericho in the spring of 4 BC. The child Jesus, however, escaped to Egypt and lived. In one sense there was nothing surprising about the death of Herod: it is a biological fact that old men die, whereas normally babies live and grow up. But the death of Herod also symbolized a philosophical truth developed above all by John in the book of Revelation that God is on his throne and that he will have the last word.

In every century there have been Herods who, recognizing the incarnate Son of God as a threat to all that they have stood for, have sought to murder him in his cradle. There was Herod's grandson, Herod Agrippa I, who tried to persecute the infant church out of existence. He killed James, the brother of John (Acts 12:2). He imprisoned Peter, intending to execute him also (Acts 12:3). He became drunk with illusions of his own divinity (Acts 12:22). But in the end he was eaten up with worms and died (Acts 12:23). Herod died; Jesus lived.

In the first three centuries a succession of 'Herods' sat on various world thrones, devising all sorts of fiendish schemes to kill off the church. Nero, for instance, ordered Christians to be wrapped up in the hides of wild beasts and torn to bits by dogs; others he nailed to crosses, while he tarred yet others and then set fire to their bodies to illuminate a circus staged for the crowds in his gardens. Yet in the end this 'Herod' died and Jesus lived. As early as AD 403 Jerome wrote: 'Even in Rome itself paganism is left in solitude. Every pagan temple in Rome is now covered with cobwebs. They who once were the gods of the nations remain under their leaking, lonely roofs with horned owls and other birds of the night.'[24]

And so the story has gone on. Adolf Hitler was in many ways a reincarnation of Herod. He threw many a faithful German Christian into his concentration camps. In the end 'Herod' died, but Jesus lives. Idi Amin was another Herod too, killing and persecuting many a faithful Ugandan Christian. This Herod died too, but Jesus lives.

Not all Herods employ the crude and violent methods of Herod the Great. Some seek to smother Jesus by creating a climate of cynicism and ridicule, and in this way destroy the Christian church. We sometimes feel overpowered by the 'Herods' present within the media, who seek to create doubt and confusion within the minds of many faithful Christians today. But if the story of Herod has anything to say, we have only to wait for God to finish the story: Herod will die and Jesus will live!

An overview: Who is Jesus?

Matthew's account of the birth of Jesus is, above all, concerned with the identity of Jesus. In a real sense, his first two chapters are simply an elaboration of his very first verse: Jesus is 'the Messiah, the son of David, the son of Abraham'.

I like the suggestion that Matthew's account of the birth of Jesus

---

24. Quoted by Leonard Griffith, *Gospel Characters* (London: Hodder & Stoughton, 1976), p. 32.

may be divided into four sections, each one of which answers a question relating to the person of Jesus:[25]

> 1:1–17: The complex genealogy of Jesus answers the question 'Who is Jesus?' He is the Son of Abraham, the Son of David, the Son of the Exile. He is the long-promised Messiah, the one to whom the Old Testament points.

> 1:18–25: The unusual birth of Jesus answers the question 'How did Jesus come to be the Messiah?' He is the Son of David, not through the ordinary process of human birth, but through the work of the Holy Spirit in the womb of Mary, his mother. The miracle of his birth further underlines his identity: as a result of this, Jesus is 'Emmanuel', 'God with us'.

> 2:1–12: The intriguing story of the star guiding the wise men answers the question 'Where was Jesus born?' Furthermore, Jesus' birth at Bethlehem underlines yet again his identity: the Son of David was born in Bethlehem; the son of Abraham receives homage from representatives of the Gentile world.

> 2:13–23: The flight of the family to Egypt and the return to Nazareth answer the question 'From where did Jesus come?' The Jesus who began his ministry in Galilee had in his early years relived the Exodus, for it was 'out of Egypt' that God called his Son. Jesus, the Messiah, had experience of pain, but also had hope of release to offer.

Who, then, is Jesus? This is the question that Matthew sets out to answer, not just in his first two chapters, but throughout his Gospel. This answer came to expression not least in the words of Peter at Caesarea Philippi: 'You are the Messiah, the Son of the living God' (Matt. 16:16).

This question of the identity of Jesus continues to fascinate the human mind. Who is this Jesus who outlasts all others? In 1966 John Lennon declared: 'The Beatles are more popular than Jesus Christ.'

---

25. See Brown, *The Birth of the Messiah*, pp. 53–54.

Yet today there are many people in the world who have never heard of the Beatles, let alone John Lennon.

Who is this Jesus about whom books, films and plays continue to be written: books, films and plays not just by Christians, but by non-Christians? In 2003, for instance, we saw the publication of *American Jesus: How the Son of God became a National Icon* by Boston University professor Stephen Prothero.[26] Then there was Mel Gibson's film *The Passion of the Christ*, released in 2004, which attracted such extraordinary interest around the world.

Who is this Jesus about whom people speculate? Was he, as Australian author Barbara Thiering in her 1992 best-seller *Jesus the Man* claimed, Mary Magdalene's lover?[27] Indeed, she argued that Jesus did not die on the cross. Instead, he married, fathered a family and later divorced. Or was Jesus, as American playwright Terrence McNally in his 1998 production of *Corpus Christi* suggested, a gay man with twelve disciples?[28]

No, Jesus was none of those things. As Matthew shows, he was 'the Messiah, the Son of the living God' (Matt. 16:16). Jesus was not just another prophet, just another 'religious celebrity', but God's Anointed One, God's own Son in fact. I find it significant that Jesus was not at all abashed to be described in those exalted terms. Rather he accepted Peter's declaration, just as later he accepted Thomas's worship of him as 'My Lord and my God!' (John 20:28). Then, without batting an eyelid, Jesus went on to speak about building his church on this confession of faith, building it in such a way that even death would not be able to overcome it. What a truly amazing statement. Jesus claimed to be more than a great teacher – he claimed to be more than a prophet – he claimed to be the Son of God and the Saviour of the world. He claimed that he would build a church, and that nothing in this world or the next would thwart him in that process!

C. S. Lewis highlighted the amazing nature of this claim, when he wrote:

---

26. Stephen Prothero, *American Jesus: How the Son of God became a National Icon* (New York: Farrar, Struas & Giroux, 2003).

27. Barbara Thiering, *Jesus the Man* (London: Corgi, 1993).

28. Terrence McNally, *Corpus Christi* (New York: Dramatists Play Service, 1998).

The discrepancy between the depth and shrewdness of His moral teaching and the rampant megalomania which must lie behind His theological teaching, unless He is indeed God, has never been satisfactorily got over . . . A man who was merely a man, and said the things Jesus said, would not be a great moral teacher. He would either be a lunatic – on a level with the man who says he is a poached egg – or else he would be the Devil of Hell.

In other words, a liar. Lewis went on:

You must make your choice. Either this man was, and is, the Son of God: or else a madman or something worse. You can shut Him up for a fool, you can spit at Him and kill Him as a demon; or you can fall at His feet and call Him Lord and God. But let us not come with any patronising nonsense about His being a great human teacher. He has not left that open to us. He did not intend to.[29]

---

29. C. S. Lewis, *Mere Christianity* (London: Collins Fontana, 1955), pp. 52–53.

2   The Good News according to Luke

The dedication to Theophilus (Luke 1:1–4)

*Since many have undertaken to set down an orderly account of the events
that have been fulfilled among us, just as they were handed on to us by those
who from the beginning were eyewitnesses and servants of the word, I too
decided, after investigating everything carefully from the very first, to write
an orderly account for you, most excellent Theophilus, so that you may know
the truth concerning the things about which you have been instructed.*

The truth of the Christmas story

For many, the Christmas story is little more than a fairy story, which
owes its origin in the creative imagination of early Christians. But
Luke would have been amazed at that suggestion. His account of the
birth of Jesus is preceded by his introduction to his Gospel, where he
claims to be in the business of truth. For in his address to Theophilus
he states that his intention is 'so that you may know the truth concerning the things about which you have been instructed' (1:4).

Luke in fact was writing a two-part historical work: Luke and the
Acts of the Apostles. Almost certainly he deliberately crafted his

introduction to be reminiscent of introductions used by other historians of the ancient world. In this regard a parallel is often drawn with the history of Rome by Dionysius of Halicarnassus: 'Before beginning to write I gathered information, partly from the lips of the most learned men with whom I came into contact, and partly from histories written by Romans of whom they spoke with praise.'[1] Luke was concerned for truth.

He makes it clear that his Gospel is based on trustworthy traditions and states that the material he uses was based on the evidence of 'eyewitnesses' (1:2). Given the personal nature of some of the accounts surrounding the birth of Jesus, traditions enshrined in Luke's birth narrative must ultimately be attributable to Mary herself. However, on most occasions others were present too.

These eyewitness accounts were in the first place 'handed on' (1:2) by word of mouth. Jewish society in those days was largely a non-literary society, with the result that the great mass of Jewish law and tradition was passed down by word of mouth. Many rabbis could recite the whole of the law by heart, with the result that they could have accurately rewritten the whole of the Old Testament even if every copy had been destroyed. Indeed, the Jews used to say that a good student was 'like a well-plastered cistern which never loses a drop of water'.[2]

When it came to writing a Gospel, Luke, however, was not the first to put pen to 'parchment'. As he himself says, 'Many have undertaken to set down an orderly account of the events that have been fulfilled among us' (1:1). The general consensus is that Luke had Mark before him when he wrote his Gospel, as also a sayings-collection (Q) common to both Matthew and himself. In addition, Luke had access to a number of sources not known to Mark and Matthew, including a special source relating to the birth of Jesus. The language and style present in Luke 1:5 – 2:52 are quite different from the rest of the Gospel and reflect a Semitic background. Some have even wondered

---

1. Dionysius of Halicarnassus, *Antiquitates Romanae* 1.6.1.

2. See William Barclay, *The First Three Gospels* (London: SCM Press, 1966), p. 44. Also Birger Gerhardson, *Memory & Manuscript: Oral Tradition and Written Transmission in Rabbinic Judaism and Early Christianity* (Lund: Gleerup, 1961).

whether Luke was translating a Hebrew or Aramaic document. However, it is more likely that Luke gained his material from a Palestinian source, which he then edited and incorporated into his Gospel.

Luke's account of the events surrounding the birth of Jesus is different in many respects from Matthew's account; and has, of course, no parallels in the Gospels of Mark and John. Some have found the differences between the Gospels disturbing and as a result have sought to 'harmonize' the four accounts into one. However, such Gospel 'harmonies' fail to tell the full story, and as a result of the conflation many of the insights and emphases of the Gospel writers get lost. The differences between the Gospels are for the most part easily accountable: in part these differences are present because of the different situations that the Gospel writers are addressing; and in part, as is the case of the birth narratives in particular, because of their differing sources. In fact the differences are an indication of the underlying truthfulness of the story. In this respect we can draw a parallel to modern newspapers, where the same story can receive very different coverage: in part because of the readership being addressed, but also in part because of the different sources available to the reporters.

It is important to emphasize that Luke treated his sources with respect. The tone of the introduction makes it clear that Luke wasn't prepared to bend the evidence to fit his theme. Luke was concerned for 'truth' (1:4). However, this does not mean that Luke was writing 'history' for 'history's sake'. Luke did not set out to write an impartial biography of Jesus; rather, like the other three evangelists, he was concerned to put over the essence of the Christian message. Luke was a 'propagandist' in the sense that he had good news to share. Luke was concerned to win over 'Theophilus'. We do not know who this Theophilus was. Bearing in mind that Luke's Gospel is part of a two-volume work, which ends with Paul about to stand trial in Rome, some have suggested that Theophilus was the examining magistrate before whom Paul was due to appear. Others maintain that Theophilus wasn't a particular individual at all, but rather that his name, which means 'friend of God', is a representative term for all who wanted to know about the Christian faith. Whoever Theophilus was, Luke wrote his Gospel to persuade people of the truth that is in Jesus, and not the least the truth that is present in the events surrounding the birth of Jesus. In this regard we should never forget that the stories of the angels and the shepherds are secondary to the good news that Jesus is the longed-for Jewish Messiah; he is the Saviour of the world; he is the Lord of all. Luke was not an impartial reporter: he had good news to share. But in sharing that good news Luke did not compromise 'truth'. Indeed, I find it significant that Luke tells us that when the disciples came to replace Judas and bring the apostolic team up to strength, nominations were restricted to those who had been 'eyewitnesses' of the life, death and resurrection of Jesus (Acts 1:21–22). Such a statement gives me confidence. The Christian faith – including the stories surrounding the birth of Jesus – are rooted in the realities of history.

The birth of Jesus foretold (Luke 1:26–38)

In the sixth month the angel Gabriel was sent by God to a town in Galilee called Nazareth, to a virgin engaged to a man whose name was Joseph, of the house of David. The virgin's name was Mary. And he came to her and said, 'Greetings, favoured one! The Lord is with you.' But she was much perplexed by his words and pondered what sort of greeting this might be. The angel said to her, 'Do not be afraid, Mary, for you have found favour with God. And now, you will conceive in your womb and bear a son, and you will name him Jesus. He will be great, and will be called the Son of the Most High, and the Lord God will give to him the throne of his ancestor David. He will reign over the house of Jacob forever, and of his kingdom there will be no end.' Mary said to the angel, 'How can this be, since I am a virgin?' The angel said to her, 'The Holy Spirit will come upon you, and the power of the Most High will overshadow you; therefore the child to be born will be holy; he will be called Son of God. And now, your relative Elizabeth in her old age has also conceived a son; and this is the sixth month for her who was said to be barren. For nothing will be impossible with God.' Then Mary said, 'Here am I, the servant of the Lord; let it be with me according to your word.' Then the angel departed from her.

Mary discovers she is having a baby!
Mary has been described as 'the best supporting character' in 'the

greatest drama ever played on the stage of history', the drama of which Jesus was the star.[3] Unfortunately, we know so little about her. The first time she appears on the stage of history she is 'engaged to a man whose name was Joseph, of the house of David' (1:27). As we have already seen in our study of Matthew's Gospel, in Jewish society of that day 'engagement' or 'betrothal' was a much more serious affair than in our society. In first-century Palestine betrothal was quite as binding as marriage itself, and could be dissolved only by divorce. Should the man to whom the girl was betrothed die, then in the eyes of the law she became a widow. It was no exaggeration to say that nothing but death could normally break a betrothal.

Mary had probably not even reached her teens, for betrothal normally took place in a girl's thirteenth year. She would still have been living at home in Nazareth with her parents. It was only at the end of the customary year-long betrothal that girls were then taken into the home of their husbands; it was only then too that sexual relationships began. Like any other girl at her stage, Mary was a 'virgin', a fact that is highlighted by Luke in his account: twice in verse 27 he mentions that Mary was a virgin; and this is repeated yet again in verse 34.

It was in the sixth month of her cousin Elizabeth's pregnancy that the angel Gabriel appeared to Mary. Gabriel is only one of two angels actually named in the Bible (the other is Michael). In Jewish angelology he was deemed to be one of the archangels who stand before God's throne (see 1:19). It is presumably with a direct message from God that Gabriel comes to Mary.

Gabriel prefaces his message by stressing the privilege that is about to be bestowed on Mary: 'Greetings, favoured one!' (1:28). Mary, says the angel, you are in receipt of God's favour; and the clear implication is that this favour is undeserved. It is all of grace (the Greek word 'favoured', *kecharitomenē*, has at its root the Greek word for 'grace', *charis*). Unfortunately, the Latin Vulgate version of the Bible understood Mary as deserving God's favour: 'Hail Mary, full of grace', which led Roman Catholics to believe that God chose Mary to

---

3. Leonard Griffith, *Gospel Characters* (London: Hodder & Stoughton, 1976), p. 11.

be the mother of Jesus because of the special grace that was hers. So Pope Pius IX declared: 'This solemn and unparalleled salutation, heard at no other time, shows the Mother of God as the seat of all divine graces, and as adorned with all the gifts of the Spirit.' From this misinterpretation of the text arose the belief in Mary's immaculate conception: namely, it was Mary's unique experience of grace that preserved her from original sin and from sinning during her life. Furthermore, Roman Catholics came to believe that as a result of her fullness of grace Mary is able to dispense grace to others. But the underlying Greek doesn't admit of such interpretation. Mary was just an ordinary village girl, whom God in his grace had chosen.

To be fair, it has not simply been Roman Catholics who have sought to find a reason for God's choice of Mary. Was she, for instance, particularly devout? Or was she particularly warm-hearted and loving? Or did she exhibit a wisdom beyond her years? In the final analysis there is no real reason why God should have chosen her. In no way did she deserve to be the mother of God. It was all of grace. And what is true of Mary is true of us all, God's grace is always unmerited. Interestingly, the only other place in the New Testament where the same word 'favoured' appears is in Ephesians 1:6: there it is used of all Christians who have experienced the forgiving grace that God 'freely bestowed on us in the Beloved'. God's actions are always all of grace.

No wonder Mary is 'much perplexed by his words' (1:29). And no doubt she is even more perplexed as Gabriel delivers his message. For the particular favour that Mary is to experience is that she will conceive and give birth to a son, whom she will name 'Jesus' (The Lord saves!): 'He will be great, and will be called the Son of the Most High, and the Lord God will give to him the throne of his ancestor David. He will reign over the house of Jacob forever, and of his kingdom there will be no end' (1:32–33). What an amazing message! Every woman believes her firstborn to be special, but Mary's child is in another league. He is to be the long-awaited Messiah, who will come and free God's oppressed people. And whereas in popular thought it was envisaged that the Messiah's reign would only be temporary and would come to an end when the kingdom of God was ushered in, here the rule of Jesus is associated with the rule of God himself.

Mary's first thought, however, is not about the identity of her son, but rather about the fact that she is to give birth to a son: 'How can this be, since I am a virgin?' (1:34); literally, 'since I do not know a man'. For Mary the thought of having a child during her year of betrothal is unthinkable. And so it is. For what is clearly implied here is virgin birth, and virgin births simply do not happen in the real world. Mary knows that; so too do Luke and his readers. Scepticism about the virgin birth is no modern phenomenon. True, the ancient world knew nothing of X and Y chromosomes, but they did know that babies are the result of men and women coming together in sexual intercourse.

Gabriel doesn't attempt to rationalize the process of virgin birth. Instead he assigns all responsibility to God: 'The Holy Spirit will come upon you, and the power of the Most High will overshadow you' (1:35). Unlike Greek legends, which depict the gods ravishing attractive young females, there is nothing sexual about God's creative activity here. Just as the Spirit was active in the creation of the world (Gen. 1:2), so here he is active in a new creation. The fact that the child to be born will be called the 'Son of God' has nothing to do with physical origin: in Jewish thought the notion of divine sonship is generally focused on adoption or election to a special relationship with God (see, for instance, the key text of 2 Samuel 7:14 that under-lies this passage). Gabriel then goes on to give an instance of the creative power of God. He points to the unusual fact of Elizabeth's pregnancy: she was both old and infertile, and yet she is already six months pregnant. This in itself is a sign of God's ability to surprise: 'For nothing will be impossible with God' (1:37). Almost certainly there is a reference back to the story of Sarah's sceptical reaction on being promised a son in her old age: the Lord rebuked her and declared: 'Is anything too wonderful for the Lord?' (Gen. 18:14). True, Sarah and Mary were in very different positions: Sarah was too old, whereas Mary was – in effect – too young. Yet God did the seemingly impossible in both their lives.

Unlike Sarah, Mary didn't laugh. She quietly accepted God's will for her life: 'Here am I, the servant of the Lord; let it be with me according to your word' (1:38). In one sense she recognized that she had no option: for as God's servant (literally, his 'slave': *doulos*), his wish was her command. And yet Mary was no puppet on a string.

She could have rejected God's calling on her life. Instead, she says her 'Yes' to God's initiative of grace. Whereupon the angel Gabriel departs, his mission accomplished.

God surprises

There are, then, four possible themes for the preacher. First, the theme of God's extraordinary ability to surprise us. 'Nothing will be impossible with God' (1:37). These words sum up the birth stories of both John the Baptist and of Jesus. Zechariah and Elizabeth were well past the time of having children, so much so that when Gabriel foretold the birth of John, Zechariah refused to believe. Even more extraordinary was the birth of Jesus: a virgin birth is inconceivable. But what was true of John the Baptist and Jesus was true of the life and ministry of Jesus: the miracle of feeding the 5,000 and of turning water into wine, the healing of the sick and the raising of the dead, and above all the resurrection of Jesus on the third day. With God all these apparently impossible acts become possible. But the ascension did not mark the end of God's mighty acts. As Luke goes on to show in the book of Acts, the gift of the Spirit and the formation of a new community, the release of captive apostles and the spread of the gospel to the ends of the earth; with God all these too became possible. And, of course, the age of miracles is not over: God still involves himself in his world and among his people. In the words of Paul: God 'by the power at work within us is able to accomplish abundantly far more than all we can ask or imagine' (Eph. 3:20). Here is a challenge to our expectancy. The degree to which God will surprise us, let alone the sceptical world outside the church, is the degree to which we give room to the Spirit to work in our lives and in his church.

All of grace

A second theme is that of grace. God in his grace chose Mary to be the mother of our Lord. In contrast with Zechariah and Elizabeth, who are described as being righteous and blameless before the Lord, who keep God's commandments and pray to the Lord, nothing is said by Luke about Mary's virtues, or indeed about her vices. Mary was just an ordinary girl. But as the apostle Paul pointed out to the church at Corinth, it is precisely the ordinary people whom God so often uses: 'Consider your own call, brothers and sisters: not many of you were wise by human standards, not many were powerful, not many were of noble birth. But God chose what is foolish in the world; . . . what is weak in the world; . . . what is low and despised in the world' (1 Cor. 1:26–28). As God in his grace called Mary to serve his purposes of redemption, so too God in his grace calls us. God is not looking for us to prove ourselves before he calls us; rather, our task is to prove ourselves once he has called us.

The response of faith

Closely following the theme of grace is the theme of faith. Mary's response to the grace of God was a mark of faith: 'Here am I, the servant of the Lord; let it be with me according to your word' (1:38). Mary exemplified the old Sunday school acronym for faith: 'forsaking all I trust him'. She was willing to trust God, whatever happened. She was willing to believe that God could use her, however inadequate she may have felt. What was true of Mary needs to be true of us. We too need to be willing to respond to the call of God on our lives, whatever that may be, however inadequate we may feel. In this regard some words of Martin Luther, inscribed over the Lutheran seminary at Wittenberg, are instructive: 'Let no one give up the faith that God wants to do a deed in him.' There is more to faith than simply saying the creed; faith involves risk, faith involves handing over our lives and their future to God.

The costliness of obedience

Finally, there is the theme of the costliness of obedience. For Mary's acceptance of God's call upon her life was to lead to shame and disgrace. Her neighbours would undoubtedly have been scandalized when they learnt that she was expecting a baby while still only engaged, and all the more if they had learnt that Joseph was not the father. No doubt Joseph exchanged strong words with her. Indeed, Matthew tells us that he considered breaking the engagement once he discovered that she was pregnant. And that was just the beginning of the costly path that Mary was to tread. The fact is that although her cousin Elizabeth addressed her as 'Blessed are you among women' (1:42), that blessedness was to be a sword to pierce her heart. For that blessedness meant that one day she would see her son hanging on a cross. The accepting of God's will for her life was costly for Mary; and what was true for Mary is also true for us. Yes, in Christ God has wonderfully blessed us: in him we have discovered forgiveness of sin and hope of eternal life. But these blessings do not necessarily lead to a path of ease. Jesus talked about his followers taking up a cross. Alas, too many of us want the pearl of great price without having to give our all. But as Mary discovered, there is pain in blessing.

Mary visits Elizabeth (Luke 1:39–45)

In those days Mary set out and went with haste to a Judean town in the hill country, where she entered the house of Zechariah and greeted Elizabeth. When Elizabeth heard Mary's greeting, the child leapt in her womb. And Elizabeth was filled with the Holy Spirit and exclaimed with a loud cry, 'Blessed are you among women, and blessed is the fruit of your womb. And why has this happened to me that the mother of my Lord comes to me? For as soon as I heard the sound of your greeting, the child in my womb leapt for joy. And blessed is she who believed that there would be a fulfilment of what was spoken to her by the Lord.'

The mothers' meeting!

Why did Mary visit her cousin, and visit her with such haste? Some have suggested that she went to check out the truth of the angel's statement that her cousin Elizabeth, childless for so many years, was already six months pregnant. But Luke's account makes it clear that Mary had already accepted Gabriel's word as true. Others have suggested she went to prevent the neighbours in Nazareth from knowing about her own pregnancy, for it was no easy thing being a single mum in such a society. This is an interesting possibility, but we have no proof. It is much more likely that Mary had a secret she was simply bursting to tell someone: 'I'm having baby! Isn't it just so exciting?' Unfortunately, the circumstances surrounding the conception of Jesus were such that she couldn't have shared this news with all and sundry. So what better thing than to go and visit her older cousin, Elizabeth, and gain from her perhaps some spiritual wisdom and understanding?

When Mary came through the door and greeted her cousin and

husband, Elizabeth experienced something quite different from the normal movement of an unborn child: 'the child leapt in her womb' (1:41). In a way that is difficult to understand, her unborn baby sensed that he was in the very presence of God. Is it too much to believe that here we have the fulfilment of what the angel had promised Zechariah, that his son, John, would be 'even before his birth . . . filled with the Holy Spirit' (1:15)? Here on this occasion John the Baptist was already taking on the role of a prophet!

Whereupon Elizabeth bursts into a song of unrestrained joy: 'Blessed are you among women, and blessed is the fruit of your womb. And why has this happened to me, that the mother of my Lord comes to me?' (1:42–43). Instead of Elizabeth pointing to her own condition, she points to Mary's. Instead of the expected mutual congratulation, all the concentration is on Mary and on her privileged pregnancy.

Putting Jesus first

Much is made of Mary's humility, and rightly so. And yet, on this occasion when the two mothers get together, it is Elizabeth's humility that is all the more striking. For Elizabeth allowed her pregnancy to be overshadowed by Mary's. On purely rational grounds, there would have been a case for Elizabeth's pregnancy getting the attention, for hers was more advanced and, as an older mother, it was more risky. But as it was, she concentrated on Mary and her pregnancy. Search as we may, we discover not a trace of jealousy. This is all the more remarkable when one realizes that Elizabeth happily acknowledges that Mary's son will be far more important than her son. Normally, parents love to brag about their own children, but not Elizabeth. Instead, Elizabeth humbly recognizes that Mary is 'the mother of my Lord' (1:43). Her humility is reminiscent of her son's humility, who later said of Jesus to his disciples, 'He must increase, but I must decrease' (John 3:30).

Our situation today is very different. We live the other side of the cross and resurrection. We know that Jesus is the Son of God, the Saviour of the world, and the Lord of life. We have no difficulty in honouring Jesus for who he is and what he is done. Or do we? If we are honest, we often struggle to give him the place that is rightly his. We often put ourselves, our families and our interests before Jesus, not least in the run-up to celebrating our Saviour's birth. Like Elizabeth, we need to allow Jesus to take centre stage.

Mary's song of praise (Luke 1:46–55)

And Mary said,

> '*My soul magnifies the Lord,*
>   *and my spirit rejoices in God my Saviour,*
> *for he has looked with favour on the lowliness of his servant.*
>   *Surely, from now on all generations will call me blessed;*
> *for the Mighty One has done great things for me,*
>   *and holy is his name.*
> *His mercy is for those who fear him*
>   *from generation to generation.*
> *He has shown strength with his arm;*
>   *he has scattered the proud in the thoughts of their hearts.*
> *He has brought down the powerful from their thrones,*
>   *and lifted up the lowly;*
> *he has filled the hungry with good things,*
>   *and sent the rich away empty.*
> *He has helped his servant Israel,*
>   *in remembrance of his mercy,*
> *according to the promise he made to our ancestors,*
>   *to Abraham and to his descendants for ever.*'

God chooses nobodies

Most mothers are excited when they know a baby is on the way. Mary wouldn't have been human if she too hadn't experienced similar excitement. But the song Mary sang was not inspired by the thought of impending motherhood, but by the growing sense of wonder that God should have chosen her to play a role in his purposes. This is why Mary sang:

> My soul magnifies the Lord,
>   and my spirit rejoices in God my Saviour,
> for he has looked with favour on the lowliness of his servant.

> Surely, from now on all generations will call me blessed;
> for the Mighty One has done great things for me. (1:46–49)

Mary was amazed that God had chosen her, an ordinary village girl, to be the mother of his Son. And rightly so. It was amazing that God should have 'looked with favour on the lowliness of his servant' (1:48), one who was right at the bottom of the pecking order. From a Jewish point of view, if God were to enter the world in the way he did, he might have been expected to have chosen the wife of one of the Sadducean priestly elite, somebody perhaps well connected with Caiaphas, the high priest and his cronies. But as it was, he chose a 'nobody' like Mary. Similarly, from a Roman point of view, it would have seemed natural for God's Son to have been born in Rome, the imperial city, rather than in some provincial backwater; furthermore, it would have made much more sense for his Son to have been born into a distinguished Roman senatorial family rather than into an obscure peasant family who were part of an odd and obstinate nation. But amazingly, God chose a 'nobody' like Mary. No wonder Mary sang her *Magnificat*. Eugene Peterson expresses well this sense of amazement and excitement in his paraphrase 'I'm bursting with God-news; I'm dancing the song of my Saviour God. God took one good look at me, and look what happened – I'm the most fortunate woman on earth!' (*The Message*).

What was true of Mary is, by extension, true of us. God's choice of us is – to put it mildly – surprising. It is amazing that we, who are but ordinary creatures bound within space and time, should be the objects of the love of God who is beyond space and time. For although we may regard ourselves as people worth loving, the brutal truth is that there is no earthly reason why God should love us. In the light of eternity we are but 'nobodies'. And yet 'God our Saviour' has loved us and sent his Son for us. With Mary, we too can say 'the Mighty One has' indeed 'done great things for us' (1:49). So let's sing our own *Magnificats* and in so doing let us note that 'magnify' the Lord does not mean that we are making God any bigger. God cannot be greater, more magnificent or more glorious than he already is. We can only testify to the glory and greatness that are already there. To magnify is to worship God; it is to acknowledge his worth.

As was the case with Mary, so too with us there is a place for excitement, amazement, wonder at the love of God for us 'nobodies'. Sadly, we are sometimes far too cool and offhand with God. True, we don't want to be people of mere 'froth and bubble': we want to be people of substance too. But once we have begun to grasp something of the substance of God's love, we have no choice. We have to express feeling and emotion. Not to do so would not be human. Loving the Lord our God with all our mind always leads on to loving him with all our heart. It's natural; it's right; it's proper.

God sides with nobodies

Overwhelmed by the fact that God has chosen her to be the mother of his Son, Mary then turned to think of her child to be. Like any other mother, Mary dreamt of great things for her son. And what dreams they were. Little did she know that not only would 'all generations' call her 'blessed', but that one of her names would also be 'Our Lady of Sorrows'. Inspired by the visit of the angel Gabriel and his message that her son would be God's Messiah, she sang of the coming revolution of which her son was to be the leader. And what a revolution it was to be! Indeed, measured by the reality of the situation in which Mary found herself, it has been said that 'the dimensions of hope have a touch of megalomania'.[4] Karl Marx would have uttered a loud 'Amen' to the thought of the powerful being brought down from their thrones, and the lowly being lifted up; of the hungry being filled with good things, and the rich being sent away. So certain was Mary of the coming revolution that she spoke of the future as if it had already arrived: we have here what is called a 'prophetic past'. The very fact that God was causing her to conceive a baby was in itself a sign that the revolution had already started.

Mary was a child of her time and so too were her dreams. The hopes she expressed were very much the popular hopes of the day. The coming Messiah was going to be a powerful political figure who would restore the fortunes of the people of God. But Mary saw through a glass darkly. Far from Jesus putting down the mighty from

---

4. Dorothee Soelle and Luise Schottroff, *Jesus of Nazareth* (ET London: SPCK, 2002), p. 12. They also point out that at that time 99% of the population could be called poor.

their thrones, they put him down. Although the life and teachings of Jesus have inspired subsequent social revolutions, in his day Jesus was a failed social revolutionary. But, as the Gospels and indeed the rest of the New Testament make clear, Jesus came to bring about a spiritual revolution: he came not to redistribute wealth, but rather to deal with sin, which is at the root of all this world's problems. In this sense Mary was wrong: Jesus did not fulfil her expectations.

And yet Mary was not totally wrong. We cannot simply spiritualize the *Magnificat*, so that it has no social or political sting at all. On the contrary: precisely because of the value that Jesus throughout his ministry gave to the poor and the marginalized, the world of politics and economics of necessity become of concern to the Christian. But there is an even deeper reason for Christians to side with the nobodies of this world, well illustrated by the story of Muretus, a poor scholar in the Middle Ages who wandered from place to place.[5] In one Italian town he fell ill and was taken to a hospital for the poor. As Muretus lay in his bed he heard the doctors discussing his case in Latin: one of them, not dreaming that Muretus could understand what they were saying, suggested that they might use this worthless wanderer for medical experiments. At this point Muretus looked up and answered them in Latin: 'Call no man worthless for whom Christ died.' How right he was: in God's sight nobody is worthless. In that sense the *Magnificat* was prophetic of the revolution Jesus did start. For no other religion has cared for others as has the Christian faith; no other religion has been as concerned for issues of justice and of peace as has the Christian faith. But the revolution that Jesus started still needs to go on: for inequality and injustice still abound. So *Vive la Revolution!* And in Christ's name let's side with the nobodies of this world!

Zechariah's prophetic song (Luke 1:67–79)

Then his father Zechariah was filled with the Holy Spirit and spoke this prophecy:

---

5. Quoted by William Barclay, *The Gospel of Luke*, Daily Study Bible (Edinburgh: St Andrew Press, 3rd ed., 1956), p. 10.

'Blessed be the Lord God of Israel,
  for he has looked favourably on his people and redeemed them.
He has raised up a mighty saviour for us
  in the house of his servant David,
as he spoke through the mouth of his holy prophets from of old,
  that we would be saved from our enemies and from the hand
    of all who hate us.
Thus he has shown the mercy promised to our ancestors,
  and has remembered his holy covenant,
the oath that he swore to our ancestor Abraham,
  to grant us that we, being rescued from the hands of our enemies,
might serve him without fear, in holiness and righteousness
  before him all our days.
And you, child, will be called the prophet of the Most High;
  for you will go before the Lord to prepare his ways,
to give knowledge of salvation to his people
  by the forgiveness of their sins.
By the tender mercy of our God,
  the dawn from on high will break upon us,
to give light to those who sit in darkness and in the shadow of death,
  to guide our feet into the way of peace.'

Blessed be God: Benedictus!

The birth of a first child calls for special celebration, especially when the child has been long awaited. So it is not surprising that the birth of his son causes Zechariah to burst into song. But it was a song with a difference: for in his song he focuses not so much on his son, but on God. The *Benedictus*, as this song is known (after the opening word of the Latin translation), is a song of praise to the God who has come to the aid of his people: God has set them free.

Most people, even if they don't go to church, believe in God. Atheism is actually a minority view. But the context of this belief in God can vary. For many, belief in God is limited to believing that somewhere behind this universe stands some power that has brought it into being. By contrast, Zechariah believed in a God who actively cared for his people.

'He has looked favourably on his people and redeemed them' (1:68). For people like Theophilus, for whom Luke wrote his Gospel, this was a revolutionary thought. The educated gentry of Luke's day believed in the god of the philosophers, a cold passionless god, a god who was beyond joy and sorrow, a god who looked down on his creatures in calm and cool detachment. But this is not the Christian God: our God is a God of passion, a God who loves and cares, who comes to the aid of his people.

In particular, Zechariah believed that God had come to the aid of his people in providing a Saviour: 'he has raised up a mighty saviour for us in the house of his servant David' (1:69). Literally, God has 'raised up a horn of salvation': this strange Semitic expression was rooted in the belief that the strength of an animal lay in its horn; the 'horn' therefore became a synonym for strength. The series of past tenses might seem strange, for Jesus had not been born when Zechariah burst into song. But Zechariah saw that in the coming of John, God had begun to work out his plan of salvation.

This theme of the plan of salvation Zechariah works out in the succeeding verses. He mentions four separate occasions when God said that he would come to the aid of his people. The coming of Jesus, in fact, fulfils what was predicted by the prophets, was promised to past generations of believers, was agreed at Mount Sinai when the covenant was concluded, and was promised to Abraham when God made a solemn oath (1:70–74). There must have been many times when it seemed God was not keeping his promise. Life, for instance, was difficult for the Jewish nation during the exile in Babylon; life continued to be difficult after the return from Babylon. But God had a plan, and the coming of Jesus was a key part of that plan. Although Zechariah did not realize it, God's plan of salvation is still in the process of being worked out. As Christians, we look forward to the day when God brings all things under the headship of Christ (see Eph. 1:10). God is indeed to be blessed!

The light has dawned

The translation of verse 78 is a little complex. Zechariah is probably likening God's salvation to 'the morning sun from heaven' (NEB)[6]

---

6. REB is similar: 'the dawn from heaven will break upon us, to shine on those who live in darkness'.

rising and giving light at the beginning of the day. However, it is possible that the reference is not to the sun, but to a bright star. It may be that Zechariah is referring to Numbers 24:17 where we read, 'a star shall come out of Jacob', imagery that was later taken up and applied to Christ in the book of Revelation: 'I am the root and descendant of David, the bright morning star' (Rev. 22:16).

Whatever the precise meaning here, the general thrust is clear. With Jesus light has come into the world, light to those who 'sit in darkness and in the shadow of death' (1:79). In a very real sense death casts a shadow on all of life. True, while we are young, we are not so conscious of its shadow. As the French philosopher, Jean Paul Sartre, said in an interview with the *Observer* newspaper: 'At one time I thought myself immortal – up to the age of 30.'[7] But with the passing of the years death begins to raise its gloomy head. Most people find the only way they can cope with it is to try not to think about it. With reason, death has been described as 'the great human repression, the universal complex . . . the reality that man dare not face and to escape which he summons all his resources'.[8] Even at the time of a funeral, when death stares them in the face, many seek escape in a vague mist of religious sentimentalism. But the good news is that because of Jesus' coming into the world we can face up to death. He has come to 'give light to those who sit in darkness and in the shadow of death'. The fact is, that without Jesus we are lost in the dark; without Jesus death is the great unknown. But with Jesus, life gains direction; death is not the end; Jesus leads us to God.

Here is good news to receive. But it is also good news to share. Zechariah speaks of his son fulfilling the calling of a 'prophet', one who would 'go before the Lord to prepare his ways' (1:76). The Jews believed that before the Messiah came, there would be a 'forerunner' who would prepare the way by announcing his coming. And this John did. He gave 'knowledge of salvation to his people by the forgiveness of their sins' (1:77) by pointing others to Jesus, saying: 'Here is the Lamb of God who takes away the sin of the world' (John 1:29). Here, in turn, is a challenge to us. John told others of the Saviour: so

---

7. *Observer Review*, 6 July 1975.

8. H. P. Lovell Cocks, quoted by Salter, *Life and Death* (Scripture Union), p. 13.

too should we. Just as Zechariah could not contain himself over the birth of his son, never should we be able to contain ourselves over the birth of the Saviour!

The census (Luke 2:1–2)

In those days a decree went out from Emperor Augustus that all the world should be registered. This was the first registration and was taken while Quirinius was governor of Syria.

Fact and not fiction

Luke begins his account of the birth of Jesus by setting it within a clear historical framework. At that time Octavian, who as a result of his victory over Anthony at the Battle of Actium was called the 'August One' (Augustus), sat on the imperial throne. He reigned as emperor from 27 BC to his death in AD 14, when he was succeeded by Tiberius (3:1).

No doubt, first and foremost, Luke was concerned to show that he was engaging with fact, not with fiction. The Christmas story is no fairy tale. The birth of Jesus and the census that caused Joseph and Mary to make their way to Bethlehem are rooted in historical reality.

In the Roman Empire periodical censuses were taken with the double object of assessing taxation and discovering those who were liable for compulsory military service. The Jews were exempt from military service and therefore in Palestine a census would have been for taxation purposes. Although we have no evidence of a formal decree from Augustus ordering that all the citizens of the empire should be registered on such-and-such a date, we do have plenty of evidence from Roman historians such as Tacitus and Suetonius that Augustus had a policy of keeping statistics on direct and indirect taxation, statistics that could only have been derived from censuses.[9] It seems that the census to which Luke refers was part of a general policy of Augustus to ensure that the whole empire was assessed for taxation purposes. Indeed, in the original Greek text Luke uses a

---

9. See Tacitus, *Annals* 1.11; Suetonius, *Life of Augustus* 94.

present tense, which suggests that this particular census that affected Joseph and Mary was part of an ongoing activity: the census, which had previously been going on in other parts of the empire, was now extended to Judea. Certainly we have evidence that a census of the whole Roman Empire was accomplished for the first time in history under Augustus.

From Josephus, the Jewish historian, we also have evidence of a provincial census undertaken by Quirinius, the governor of Syria, a census that caused the Jews to revolt in protest against what they perceived to be a form of economic slavery. The difficulty, however, is that this particular census took place around AD 6, a good number of years after the death of King Herod in 4 BC. Luke, therefore, must have been referring to an earlier census. Since censuses normally took place every fourteen years, we can work out that this earlier census took place in 8 BC. But some have questioned whether Quirinius was involved in that earlier census, since he did not become governor of Syria until AD 6. On the other hand, inscriptions on public buildings appear to indicate that from 10 to 7 BC Quirinius performed military functions in the Roman province of Syria before he returned to become governor of Syria and could well have been involved in the organization of that earlier census. Indeed, the wording that is found in 2:2 is a little unusual: grammatically, it is quite possible to translate Luke's statement as: 'This census took place before Quirinius actually became governor of Syria.' All the evidence points clearly to the historicity of a census taking place at the time of the birth of Jesus.

But did Joseph and Mary really have to travel down to Bethlehem to take part in the census? It has been suggested that a Roman census would not have required Joseph and Mary to travel to their ancestral home for registration, and that in any case it is improbable that the Romans would have undertaken such a census in a client state like Judea, which already had Herod as its own ruler. However, if we understand the census as being in line with the overall policy of Augustus, there is no reason why Herod should not have conducted a census along traditional Jewish lines, which may well have necessitated people returning to their ancestral homes.

There is, therefore, no overwhelming reason why we should doubt the veracity of Luke's account. It is entirely plausible that

Joseph and Mary did indeed go to Bethlehem in order to register themselves.

All this is not surprising, since Luke in his introduction to his Gospel makes it clear that he sets out to be a historian. Christianity is a historical religion. The incarnation actually happened, and as a result the world has not been the same since. This is important, for ultimately the Christian faith is based not on a set of ideas, but a series of events. Books on the Christian faith are not to be catalogued under philosophy, but under history. As C. S. Lewis once wrote: 'If Christianity only means one more bit of good advice, then Christianity is of no importance. There has been no lack of good advice for the last four thousand years. A bit more makes no difference.'[10] At Christmas we celebrate the birth not of an idea, but of a child, who is Christ the Lord. In the words of Zechariah, we need to face the fact that God 'has provided for us a mighty Saviour'.

False and true hope

Yet is it possible that there is another theme present within these two verses, a theme of false over against true hope? Certainly, one cannot but mark the contrast between Augustus and Jesus.

When Augustus assumed the throne, it was a time of great hope. After all the bloodshed that had followed the assassination of Julius Caesar, a new age of peace was about to begin. As we noted earlier, in 40 BC the Roman poet Virgil had written his *Fourth Eclogue* in which he spoke of a golden age, in which the harmony of nature would be restored and in which sin and guilt would be removed: to the minds of many those hopes had found their realization in Augustus. To symbolize the peace that Augustus had brought, there was erected in Rome the great altar of peace (Ara Pacis Augustae). The Greek cities of Asia Minor, perhaps not far from where Luke was writing, adopted Augustus' birthday, 23 September, as the first day of the new year, calling him a 'saviour'; indeed, an inscription at Halicarnassus calls him 'saviour of the whole world'. In the words of the 'Priene' inscription:

---

10. C. S. Lewis, *Mere Christianity* (London: Collins Fontana, 1955), pp. 132–133.

Providence has ordered our life in a divine way . . . the Emperor through his epiphany has exceeded the hopes of former good news, surpassing not only the benefactors who came before him, but also leaving no hope that anyone in the future will surpass him . . . the birthday of the god has marked the beginning of the good news for the world.

The nearest parallel we in the UK have to this phenomenon in modern times was the return of Labour to power in 1996 after so many years of being in opposition. The arrival of Tony Blair in Downing Street was greeted with much enthusiastic flag-waving. The old Tory era was over; a new era had arrived. At that time great hopes were invested in Tony Blair and his government.

But as with Tony Blair, so too with Augustus, hopes were eventually dashed. In the case of Augustus, the peace the empire enjoyed proved relatively short-lived. After his death he was succeeded by Caesars who turned the Roman dream into nightmares.

It is difficult to believe that Luke was not unmindful of that dream as he wrote of the events around Jesus' birth. For the angel of the Lord used terms such as 'Saviour' and 'Lord' to describe the newborn baby Jesus, titles long familiar with the emperor cult; and the angelic choir sang of 'peace' on earth, a theme so central to the beginning of Augustus' reign. But whereas the hopes surrounding Augustus' imposing beginnings had proved to be false, the hopes surrounding the lowly birth of Jesus proved well founded. Jesus is our only true hope.

The application of this theme to our world today is surely not far to seek. It is not only politicians who peddle 'hope'. On a daily basis we are bombarded with images of well-being brought about by entering the National Lottery or taking up a bank loan, by booking a special holiday or going on the latest diet, by attending a fitness centre or by enjoying therapy of one kind or another. Over against such promises we have to proclaim that the world's true 'well-being' (*shalom*) is found in Jesus. Jesus will never disappoint.

The birth of Jesus (Luke 2:3–7)

All went to their own towns to be registered. Joseph also went from the town of Nazareth in Galilee to Judea, to the city of David called Bethlehem, because he was descended from the house and family of David. He went to be registered with Mary, to whom he was engaged and who was expecting a child. While they were there, the time came for her to deliver her child. And she gave birth to her firstborn son and wrapped him in bands of cloth, and laid him in a manger, because there was no place for them in the inn.

In Bethlehem the Saviour was born

Tax demands are never welcome, and not least when they involve a personal appearance with a tax inspector. Joseph, because he was 'descended from the house and family of David' had to put in a personal appearance in his ancestral village of Bethlehem. Bethlehem, somewhat unusually, is described as 'the city of David'. In the Old Testament, Jerusalem (not Bethlehem) was known as the 'city' or 'town' of David (see 2 Sam. 5:7, 9; 6:16; 10:12, 11:16; 2 Kgs 9:28; 12:20). However, Bethlehem was David's home town: it was there that he was born and brought up (1 Sam. 16). Furthermore, according to Micah 5:2, Bethlehem was the place from where the Messiah would emerge to 'rule in Israel'. Bethlehem was an appropriate place for Jesus to be born.

Joseph took Mary with him. It is unclear as to whether or not Mary's presence was actually required. It may be that the reason for her going up to Bethlehem was because Joseph did not want her to stay at home alone. For it would appear that by this time Mary had left her family and was living with Joseph. However, the somewhat convoluted way in which Luke describes their relationship (2:5) suggests that they had yet to embark on any sexual relationship with one another.

In modern terms the journey between Nazareth and Bethlehem was not long. It was a distance of only eighty-five miles. But it was a journey that had to be done on foot, or perhaps on a donkey. It was a journey full of hazards: for not only would Joseph and Mary have had to cope with the threat of robbers, there was also the fact that as they drew nearer to Bethlehem the terrain would have become somewhat mountainous. For a woman in the final stages of pregnancy, such a journey was quite a challenge.

It was there in Bethlehem that Mary 'gave birth to her firstborn son' (2:7). Like any other Palestinian mother, she 'wrapped him in bands of cloth'. Needless to say, the fact that Mary is depicted as doing the wrapping – as distinct from Joseph or a midwife – is not a sign that the birth was miraculous or painless. The birth was like any other birth. And no doubt Jesus was like any other baby, wizened and as full of wind as any other baby, and no doubt strong lungs to boot! No 'little Lord Jesus no crying he makes'.

But where did this all happen? The traditional interpretation of the circumstances surrounding the birth of Jesus is that, because so many people had arrived to register for the census, the inn was full, and therefore Joseph and Mary had to make do with a stable at the rear. But, there may well have been no inn in Bethlehem. After all, Bethlehem was only a small village and was not on any major road. Furthermore, when in the parable of the Good Samaritan Luke wanted to speak of an inn, he used another word (*pandocheion*, 10:34).

The fact is that the Greek word found in Luke 2:7 (*katalyma*) can be translated as 'inn', but it can also mean a 'house' or 'guest room'. Mary and Joseph were probably staying with relatives or friends, and not in an inn. If so, it may well be that it was not Mary and Joseph who were excluded from the 'house' or 'guest room', but rather only the baby Jesus: that is, they laid Jesus in a manger, because there was no space for them all in the 'house' or 'guest room'. Furthermore, the manger in question was almost certainly not outside in some barn or shed, but – as was the case with the vast majority of ancient Near Eastern peasant homes – the manger was under the same roof. The animals as well as the family slept within one large enclosed space, with the family living quarters separated by a raised platform area from the area occupied by the animals. The manger was either free-standing or attached to the wall. Mary may well have given birth to her child in the family room, and then placed him in the adjacent manger.[11]

Again, contrary to popular thinking, Luke does not necessarily

---

11. There is no mention of an ox and an ass in the stable. These animals, often shown in Nativity and Adoration scenes, are derived from the sixth-century apocryphal gospel known as Pseudo-Matthew. Their presence in Bethlehem was based on a quotation from Isa. 1:3: 'The ox knows its owner; and the donkey [AV: ass] its master's crib'.

imply that Mary was already 'full-term' when she and Joseph arrived in Bethlehem. Indeed, the opposite would appear to be the case. It was 'while they were there' (not 'upon their arrival') that Mary went into labour. The familiar image of Mary and Joseph arriving in Bethlehem and being unable to find a place to stay on the night of arrival probably has no basis in the text itself.

No room for the Saviour?

So where does this all leave the preacher? If Jesus was born in a home among friends and relatives – as distinct from being relegated to a stable because there was no room in the inn – many a good sermon disappears. In the past I have preached about the need to make room for Jesus in our hearts, Jesus who stands at the door and knocks, wanting to come in (see Rev. 3:20). I have spoken about the need to make room for him in our Christmas celebrations – for sadly we can be so busy writing cards, buying presents, cooking food and entertaining the family, that we forget 'the reason for the season'. Similarly, I have challenged congregations to make room for others in distress, whether they live in the developing world or are asylum seekers on our doorsteps, reminding them that Jesus is present in the hungry and the thirsty. For, in the words of the parable, 'just as you did it to the least of these who are members of my family, you did it to me' (Matt. 25:40). I have also reflected on the feelings of the inn-keeper who apparently turned Jesus away: 'If only he had realized who Mary's baby was to be! But he didn't. He missed his chance to be host to God's Son.' But all these sermons lose their potency if, in fact, Mary and Joseph had been staying with friends and relatives.

Born into our world

But there is another possible application. For Jesus was placed in a manger. And that manger is a sign of the mess and of the muddle into which God came. Certainly, by modern Western standards, there is no place less hygienic than an animal feeding trough. The mind boggles as one reflects on the conditions surrounding the birth of Jesus. Indeed, the newspapers reported recently that the Bishop of Horsham, Lindsay Urwin, wanted his clergy to have buckets of manure in church at Christmas-time to remind people that Jesus was born in a stable full of mess. He said: 'The incense   a symbol of divinity   together with the

smell of manure represent the paradox of the incarnation.'
Furthermore, he said, the aroma of the manure, wafting around the
church, would remind people that Jesus gave his life to clearing up the
mess men and women had made.[12]

The shepherds and the angels (Luke 2:8–20)

*In that region there were shepherds living in the fields, keeping watch over
their flock by night. Then an angel of the Lord stood before them, and the
glory of the Lord shone around them, and they were terrified. But the angel
said to them, 'Do not be afraid; for see – I am bringing you good news of
great joy for all the people: to you is born this day in the city of David a
Saviour, who is the Messiah, the Lord. This will be a sign for you: you will
find a child wrapped in bands of cloth and lying in a manger.' And suddenly
there was with the angel a multitude of the heavenly host, praising God and
saying,*

> *'Glory to God in the highest heaven,*
> *and on earth peace among those*
> *whom he favours!'*

*When the angels had left them and gone into heaven, the shepherds said
to one another, 'Let us go now to Bethlehem and see this thing that has taken
place, which the Lord has made known to us.' So they went with haste and
found Mary and Joseph, and the child lying in the manger. When they saw
this, they made known what had been told them about this child; and all
who heard it were amazed at what the shepherds told them. But Mary
treasured all these words and pondered them in her heart. The shepherds
returned, glorifying and praising God for all they had heard and seen, as it
had been told them.*

The shepherds
If we only had the story of the wise men, then it might seem that
Jesus is only of relevance to the wise and the wealthy. But the truth is

---

12. *Church Times*, 22 November 2003.

that Jesus is also of relevance to those who are not particularly wise and who have little or no money to their name.

These shepherds, Luke informs us, were 'living in the fields, keeping watch over their flock by night' (Luke 2:8): indicating that whenever else Jesus was born, he was not born on 25 December, for sheep were not kept out in the fields in the depth of winter. Sheep were kept out between March and November. Nobody knows when Jesus was born. Interestingly, around AD 200 there were two theories about the date: one was that Jesus was born on 20 May; the other, that he was born on either 20 or 21 April.

The shepherds were 'keeping watch'. Literally, they were 'watching the watches of the night': that is, they were taking turn watching over their flock by night. Probably, there were only three or four shepherds, each of them taking a turn to keep watch during the night.

As an aside we may note that it is this verse that, for popular piety, has fixed 'the night' as the time of Jesus' birth. As for the precise hour of his birth, midnight was suggested by the application of a verse from the intertestamental book of the *Wisdom of Solomon*, where we read:

> For while gentle silence enveloped all things,
> and night in its swift course was now half gone,
> your all-powerful word leaped from heaven, from the
> royal throne. (*Wisdom of Solomon* 18:14–15)

The truth is that we don't know when Jesus was born.

Who were these shepherds? Some have speculated that they were particularly godly men whose task it was to care for sheep destined to be used for sacrifice in the temple at Jerusalem. More probably they were ordinary shepherds looking after very ordinary sheep, and as such were far from being godly.

In first-century Palestine, shepherds had a reputation for being downright irreligious. They were so irreligious that they were called 'people of the dirt' 'scumbags', if you like. No self-respecting Jewish parents would have wanted their daughter to marry a shepherd. For shepherds had as much standing in the Jewish community as tax-collectors. In part this reputation was not their fault. For their job inevitably meant that they were unable to keep the Jewish ceremonial law; not for them the observance of ritual hand-washings and all the other rules and regulations practised by devout Jews. They were rough-and-ready chaps. But it wasn't only the ceremonial law that they failed to observe. They also had a reputation for not keeping the moral law. They were generally held to be thoroughly dishonest. Like some of today's 'travellers', they had an unfortunate habit of confusing 'mine' with 'thine'. Things went missing when the shepherds came to town. Furthermore, when they were out of town, they often allowed their flocks to graze upon other people's land. As a result of this reputation, no shepherd was allowed to play a part in a court of law, no shepherd could be called to act as a witness: they just couldn't be trusted!

And yet it was to shepherds that God sent the angelic choir. It was to shepherds that God made known that a Saviour was born in David's city. It was the shepherds, and not the wise men, who were the first to receive the news.

What does this say to us? Surely this: Jesus is good news for everybody! Listen again to the words of the angel: 'I am bringing you good news of great joy for *all* the people: to you is born this day in the city of David a Saviour, who is the Messiah, the Lord'. The churches may be largely the preserve of the middle classes, but Jesus is most certainly not. Jesus is the Saviour of the world. What's more, Jesus is good news not just for church-goers, but for non-church-goers. As Jesus said on more than one occasion: 'I have not come to call respectable people to repent, but sinners' (see Luke 5:32). It doesn't matter who we are or what we have done, God accepts us as we are. We don't have to reach a certain standard of holiness before God loves us, he loves us as we are. We do not have to prove ourselves.

The good news is that there is nobody outside the scope of the love of God. And to prove it, as it were, God sent the message of his Son's birth to a bunch of freewheeling shepherds spending the night in the fields, taking care of their sheep.

Joy to the world

The birth of any baby is a joyous occasion. The birth of Jesus was surely no exception. Mary and Joseph must have been overjoyed with the birth of their firstborn. True, the circumstances surrounding the birth may not have been the easiest. But at the end of the day the sur-roundings were immaterial: mother and baby were well! In the days before the rise of modern medical science this was a real blessing. Yes, there was great joy in Bethlehem that night.

But there must also have been great joy in the fields outside Bethlehem. For as the shepherds were watching their sheep, the angel of the Lord came to them with a message of good news: 'I am bringing you good news of great joy . . . to you is born this day in the city of David a Saviour, who is the Messiah, the Lord' (2:10b–11). The message, and not just the medium of the message, must have amazed them. Nobody had ever brought them good news before; indeed, they themselves were regarded by most people as 'bad news'. To be singled out by God in this way was beyond belief. Socially and religiously, they were at the bottom of the heap. Cold-shouldered by all god-fearing people because of their lifestyle, they were on nobody's guest list. But suddenly they discovered that they were on God's guest list. The doors of the synagogue may have been closed to them, but not the doors of the kingdom of God. To them a Saviour was born. Here indeed is 'good news of great joy'. Nobody is beyond the pale, as far as God is concerned. God's love is not restricted to a particular class or type of person. The ordinary as well as the important, the non-church-going as well as the church-going: all are encompassed by the love of God. It doesn't matter who we are, or what we have done. Nobody is too far gone for God. He has provided a Saviour for us all. No wonder, after visiting Mary and Joseph and their baby, the shepherds returned 'glorifying and praising God'. There was much to celebrate.

If the truth be told, some of their celebration may have been mis-placed. For when the shepherds heard of a Saviour being born in the city of David, the last thing they would have thought of was a Saviour hanging on a cross. When they heard of a Saviour, they thought of a political liberator, one who would free his people from the foreign yoke. At that time the Messiah by definition was a warrior Messiah who would overthrow the Roman power and restore Israel's fortunes. The thought of a suffering Messiah was inconceivable. It was not until after the cross and the resurrection that all this began to become clear. Had the shepherds known and understood the full extent of the salvation that Jesus came to bring, their joy would have been even greater. In the words of Peter, they would have rejoiced 'with an indescribable and glorious joy' (1 Pet. 1:8).

The 'good news of great joy' that came to the shepherds that night was not intended for them alone. It was 'for all the people'. In the first place, 'the people' concerned were the Jewish people: the expression used by the angel is a technical term for the people of God. But although Jesus may have been the long-promised Messiah who came to fulfil the hopes expressed in the Old Testament Scriptures, he also came to fulfil the hopes and aspirations of the Jewish race. As the Gospels make clear, Jesus broke through the mould of Jewish exclusivism. It is not without significance that in his version of Jesus' family tree, Luke traces the roots of Jesus back not just to David and to Abraham, but also right back to Adam (Luke 3:23–38). Jesus is no mere Jewish Messiah: he is the Saviour of the world. So Peter on the Day of Pentecost not only proclaimed that God had made Jesus both 'Lord and Messiah' (Acts 2:36), but also drew upon the prophecy of Joel to declare that 'everyone who calls on the name of the Lord shall be saved' (Acts 2:21). The 'good news of great joy' is therefore for all. So with justification we can sing America's favourite carol, 'Joy to the world, the Lord has come'.

But that night there was also joy in heaven itself. For Luke, in his account of the nativity, writes: 'And suddenly there was with the angel a multitude of the heavenly host, praising God and saying, "Glory to God in the highest heaven"' (2:13–14). What an incredible experience this must have been. It makes the most rousing rendition of the 'Hallelujah Chorus' seem pretty tame. At this pivotal stage in the history of the world's salvation, all heaven rejoiced. And heaven continues to rejoice whenever a further step is taken in the salvation of the world, for, as Jesus was later to say, 'there is joy in the presence of the angels of God over one sinner who repents' (Luke 15:10).

But preachers cannot stop there. They need to personalize the message of this 'good news of great joy' and to challenge their listeners to ensure that there is joy in their hearts too!

Good news of a Saviour from Bethlehem

Angels are not an everyday experience. So on that night of nights it was not surprising that the little group of shepherds 'were terrified' (2:9) when an angel of the Lord appeared to them in all his glory.

Precisely what lay behind that remarkable experience, we do not know. This angelic vision defies rational explanation. However, for preachers and their congregations the focus should not be on the supernatural phenomena, but on the message the angel delivered that night: 'Do not be afraid; for see – I am bringing you good news of great joy for all the people: to you is born this day in the city of David a Saviour, who is the Messiah, the Lord' (2:10–11).

For most of us the place where we were born is more or less irrelevant. About the only time we ever have to remember where we were born is when we make a passport application. But with Jesus it was different. For Jesus was born in Bethlehem. Bethlehem was supremely 'the city of David'. It was there that David was born, there that David had kept his father's sheep, and there too that the Jews expected great David's greater son to be born. Seven hundred years before the birth of Jesus the land of Judah was facing disaster: the Babylonians had destroyed Jerusalem and were taking away many of its people into exile. But Micah proclaimed that the Lord had not abandoned his people for ever. The day would come when he would rescue her from her enemies. And he would do so by means of a ruler from Bethlehem, one who traced his family line back to David (Mic. 5:2). It was therefore fitting that Jesus was born in Bethlehem, Jesus in whom the hopes and dreams of Micah were more than fulfilled.

For many centuries the Jews had looked for a saviour. The return of the Jewish exiles from Babylon had not exactly revived their fortunes. The result was that when Jesus was born, messianic fever was in the air. When any new voice rang out across the land, the question on every lip was this: 'Is this the Messiah? Are you the one who is going to save our nation from oppression? Are you the one who is going to free us from the Roman army of occupation?' The air was tense with expectation. The non-Jewish world too was looking for a saviour. People were sick of war and destruction; people longed for a golden age of peace and prosperity. Hopes were raised when Caesar Augustus came to the throne and put an end to the civil wars that had ravaged the empire after the assassination of Julius Caesar. Many thought Augustus was the saviour, the one who would usher in the age of gold. 'No,' said the angel. 'To you is born this day in the city of David a Saviour, who is the Messiah, the Lord.' The birthday worthy of divine honour, the true beginning of time, took place in Bethlehem, not in Rome.

Good news came – and still comes – from Bethlehem. This is not to say that others have nothing to offer: politicians have a role to fulfil and a job to do; computers and the electronic superhighway have revolutionized life for millions; psychotherapy and analysis, aromatherapy and massage, relieve the stress many suffer in the workplace or in the home. But none of these alternative 'saviours' offers the ultimate panacea for this world's ills. None of them can deal with the root cause of all our problems. None can deal with that infection which the Bible calls 'sin', which destroys our relationships not only with God but also with one another, and which ultimately destroys us. But Jesus can – for Jesus can save us from our sins – Jesus is the only true Saviour. Good news comes from Bethlehem.

The sign of the manger

We live in a world where status symbols are important. The designer dress, the turbocharged sports car, the Rolex watch, the Gucchi handbag: all are signs of wealth and success. How far removed all this is from the world of Jesus. The only 'sign' that the angel gave to the shepherds was that 'you will find a child wrapped in bands of cloth and lying in a manger' (2:12). This was the sign that 'a Saviour, the Messiah, the Lord' had come. What an amazing and paradoxical sign! Hardly fitting for one bearing such honoured titles!

In the first place, this was a sign of recognition. Needless to say, the key to the recognition was that Jesus was 'lying in a manger'. There was nothing unusual about the 'swaddling cloths'. Such cloths were standard in homes rich and poor. Not to wrap a baby up in such a way would have been not to care for the child. No, it was the fact that the baby was lying in a feeding trough that was significant. No fancy 'Moses basket' for this child. Instead, a first-century equivalent of an orange box. This was the sign by which the shepherds knew that they had arrived at the right place. No other family in Bethlehem would have had to resort to such a basic place for their baby.

It was too a sign of the future to come. It was a sign of the lifestyle Jesus was to adopt when he began his ministry. So to one would-be follower Jesus said: 'Foxes have holes, and birds of the air have nests; but the Son of Man has nowhere to lay his head' (Luke 9:58). Jesus, in order to fulfil his mission, sat loose to material comforts. He expects his followers to do the same: in today's status-ridden consumer society that comes as quite a shock.

Most importantly, it was a sign of the present. It was a sign of the depths to which God went in coming among us. Eight hundred or so years previously Isaiah had spoken of a 'sign' that God would give to Ahaz: 'The young woman is with child and shall bear a son, and shall name him Emmanuel' (Isa. 7:14). In a way that went beyond the wildest dreaming of Isaiah, God fulfilled that prophecy: there in the manger Emmanuel was present. The manger is an amazing sign of divine condescension. Something of the wonder of that divine condescension is reflected in the Christ-hymn of Philippians 2:

who, though he was in the form of God,
   did not regard equality with God
   as something to be exploited,
but emptied himself,
taking the form of a slave,
      being born in human likeness. (Phil. 2:6–7)

The thought of 'a Saviour, who is the Messiah, the Lord . . . lying in a manger' is almost beyond comprehension. It defies all normal human reasoning. The amazing nature of the incarnation is well described by J. B. Phillips in his fantasy 'The Visited Planet'.[13] There a senior angel is showing a very young angel the splendours of the universe. At last they come to one particular galaxy of 500 billion stars:

As the two of them drew near to the star which we call our sun and to its circling planets, the senior angel pointed to a small and rather insignificant sphere turning very slowly on its axis. It looked as dull as a dirty tennis-ball to the little angel, whose mind was filled with the size and glory of what he had seen. 'I want you to watch that one particularly,' said the senior angel pointing with his finger. 'Well, it looks very small and rather dirty to me,' said the little angel. 'What's special about that one?'

---

13. J. B. Phillips, *New Testament Christianity* (London: Hodder & Stoughton, 1958), pp. 27–33.

The little angel listened in stunned disbelief as the senior angel told him that this small, insignificant and not overclean planet was the renowned Visited Planet.

> 'Do you mean that our great and glorious Prince . . . went down in person to this fifth-rate ball? Why should He do a thing like that?' . . . The little angel's face wrinkled in disgust. 'Do you mean to tell me', he said, 'that He stooped so low as to become one of those creeping, crawling creatures of that float-ing ball?' 'I do, and I don't think that He would like you to call them "creeping, crawling creatures" in that tone of voice. For, strange as it may seem to us, He loves them. He went down to visit them to lift them up to become like Him.' The little angel looked blank. Such a thought was almost beyond his comprehension.

'This will be a sign for you: you will find a child . . . lying in a manger'. No wonder the shepherds returned, 'glorifying and praising God for all that they had heard and seen' (2:20).

The song of the angels

First and foremost the angels sing their *gloria* to God: 'Glory to God in the highest'. Luke here is using a Semitic expression to describe God as reigning 'in the highest' heaven, not suggesting that the angels have reached new heights in their praise. They praise God for the birth of his Son and for the fact that in him God was establishing a new kingdom of 'peace on earth'.

The coming of the Messiah and the coming of a new kingdom of peace went hand in hand in Jewish thinking. Centuries ago, for instance, the prophet Isaiah had described the coming Messiah as 'the Prince of Peace' (Isa. 9:6) who would usher in an age of 'endless peace' (Isa. 9:7). On that day 'all the boots of the tramping warriors and all the garments rolled in blood shall be burned as fuel for the fire' (Isa. 9:5).

But the 'peace on earth' of which the angels sang was more than an end to war. For Jews the word 'peace' (*shalom*) is a positive word, not a negative one. It is not so much a life free from the sound and fury of war as a life characterized by harmony, prosperity, joy and well-being. Peace is all that we could desire, and more!

This peace has God as its source. It is here to be enjoyed by 'those whom he favours' (2:14). At this point the NRSV, as indeed all modern translations, differs from the Authorized Version. The angels do not wish 'on earth peace' and 'good will toward men'. Nor, for that matter, do they wish 'peace to men of good will'. Rather, God offers his peace to those 'on whom his favour rests' (NIV). Who are the recipients of his favour? The context would appear to indicate that we all are. God's peace is not for the chosen few, but rather 'for all the people' to whom the good news of great joy was directed.

The good news is that God directs his favour not just to the best of us, but to the worst of us too. The fact is that none of us deserves the gift of God's love in Jesus. But God directs his favour to all. Here is cause for us to burst out with praise and with the angels sing, 'Glory to God in the highest', for God's peace is extended to us all.

The example of the shepherds
The shepherds had their failings. Their lives were far from perfect. They were doubtless rough-and-ready people. And yet their response to the angelic choir is exemplary. Would that everybody listening to a sermon were equally responsive!

First of all, they followed up what they had heard. They could have remained in the fields, marvelling at what they had just experienced. There was much to talk about. But instead, they said to one another, 'Let us go now to Bethlehem and see this thing that has taken place' (2:15). Were they at this point already 'believers'? When they set off for Bethlehem, were they already on a journey of faith? If so, then they set us an example of putting faith in action. However, it is more likely that they were still on a journey toward faith; they had yet to be convinced of the truth of what they had heard. However, they were willing to 'go and see' for themselves what this baby was all about. In so doing they set an example of honest enquiry.

Secondly, they did not delay their journey. They could have debated at length whether they should go; they could have spent time arguing about the significance of what they had just seen and heard. As it was, 'they went with haste' (2:16) to find the baby Jesus. In so doing they set an example to us. It is so easy to waste one's life away, forever talking about religion, but never actually taking the road to Bethlehem, never looking for Jesus himself. The road to hell, it has been said, is paved with good intentions: good intentions of finding out more about Jesus, but in the end never getting round to doing so.

Thirdly, they 'found Mary and Joseph, and the child lying in the manger' (2:16). Commentators often point out the significance of the word order: Mary here takes precedence over Joseph. However, of greater significance is surely that the shepherds found the child. In itself this was perhaps not a great feat. Even though numbers were swollen with people returning for the census, Bethlehem was not a large place. But nonetheless, the shepherds surely had to do some searching before they found the baby. The words of the Lord spoken through Jeremiah come to mind: 'When you search for me, you will find me; if you seek me with all your heart' (Jer. 29:13), as also the words of Jesus himself: 'search, and you will find' (Matt. 7:7). The finding does depend on the searching. The shepherds found because they put their minds to the search.

Fourthly, they told others. In the first instance they told others 'what had been told them about this child' (2:17). Here the reference is to their experience of the angels. Later on, however, they undoubtedly included the story of finding Jesus himself. And as a result, 'all who heard it were amazed at what the shepherds had told them'. In this respect too they set an example to us. They couldn't keep quiet about their experience, and in particular they couldn't keep quiet about Jesus. Would that we too found it difficult to contain ourselves!

Finally, they returned 'glorifying and praising God' (2:20). Again, what an example they set us.

A tale of two responses

When the shepherds came to Bethlehem with the news of their angelic visitation, 'all who heard it were amazed at what the shepherds told them' (2:18). It was an astonishing story, but also a story soon forgotten. A nine-day wonder perhaps, but then no more.

By contrast, Luke reports that 'Mary treasured all these words and pondered them in her heart' (2:19). Mary did not forget the story; neither did she forget any of the events of those days. Over the coming months and years she continued to think deeply over them. Only perhaps after the resurrection of Jesus did she pick up the courage to share her memories of that momentous time, and in so doing became the chief source of Luke's account of the birth of Jesus.

There is a very real contrast between the response of the ordinary village folk to the shepherds' report and Mary's. The response of the village folk is reminiscent of the response of those whom Jesus likened to rocky soil, who when they heard the word 'receive it with joy', but then, because they have no root, 'believe only for a while' (Luke 8:13). Mary's response, by contrast, is reminiscent of those whom Jesus likened to good soil, who 'when they hear the word, hold it fast in an honest and good heart, and bear fruit with patient endurance' (8:15).

Indeed, the preacher can take the Parable of the Sower as a paradigm for the differing responses to the Christmas message. There are some who can be likened to the concrete pavement on which they walk as they do their Christmas shopping. They hear the Christmas carols sung, but pay no attention to the message. They may even attend a Midnight Mass, but the words of the preacher go through one ear and out another. They do not believe, and so are not saved. Then there are others who, like the Bethlehem village folk, can be likened to rocky soil. They love to sing the Christmas carols, they always go to church at Christmas, but their response to the Christmas story is no more than skin deep. They are like the Christmas trees that decorate many a home, which have no root and so soon die. They believe for a while, but then fall away. There are yet others who can be likened to thorny soil. They are really moved by the Christmas story. Over New Year they make a resolution to go to church every week, and for a while keep that resolution. They may even attend an Alpha course and commit their life to Christ. But along come pressures of various kinds, and God gets squeezed out. Their new-found faith is soon choked to death. Finally, there are others who, like Mary, 'treasure' God's word in their heart. They not only hear God's word, but that word becomes alive in them: for Christ enters and they are born again to eternal life.

Mary 'treasured all these words and pondered them in her heart', and so must we.

The presentation of Jesus in the temple (Luke 2:22–36)

When the time came for their purification according to the law of Moses, they brought him up to Jerusalem to present him to the Lord (as it is written in the law of the Lord, 'Every firstborn male shall be designated as holy to the Lord'), and they offered a sacrifice according to what is stated in the law of the Lord, 'a pair of turtle-doves or two young pigeons'.

Now there was a man in Jerusalem whose name was Simeon; this man was righteous and devout, looking forward to the consolation of Israel, and the Holy Spirit rested on him. It had been revealed to him by the Holy Spirit that he would not see death before he had seen the Lord's Messiah. Guided by the Spirit, Simeon came into the temple; and when the parents brought in the child Jesus, to do for him what was customary under the law, Simeon took him in his arms and praised God, saying,

> *'Master, now you are dismissing your servant in peace,*
> *according to your word;*
> *for my eyes have seen your salvation,*
> *which you have prepared in the presence of all peoples,*
> *a light for revelation to the Gentiles*
> *and for glory to your people Israel.'*

And the child's father and mother were amazed at what was being said about him. Then Simeon blessed them and said to his mother Mary, 'This child is destined for the falling and the rising of many in Israel, and to be a sign that will be opposed, so that the inner thoughts of many will be revealed – and a sword will pierce your own soul too.'

There was also a prophet, Anna the daughter of Phanuel, of the tribe of Asher. She was of great age, having lived with her husband seven years after her marriage, then as a widow to the age of eighty-four. She never left the temple but worshipped there with fasting and prayer night and day. At that moment she came, and began to praise God and to speak about the child to all who were looking for the redemption of Jerusalem.

Simeon's tribute to Jesus

When Jesus was presented in the temple, two ceremonies were taking place, both of which had their roots in the Jewish law. The first of these was the ritual of purification for a mother after child-birth (2:22). Leviticus 12 laid down that a Jewish woman who gave birth to a son should, forty days after the birth, go to the temple and offer for the purposes of purification a sacrifice of a one-year-old lamb for a burnt-offering and a pigeon or a dove for a sin-offering. But if the woman cannot afford a lamb, 'she shall take two turtle-doves or two pigeons' (Lev. 2:8). Mary and Joseph were clearly hard up and couldn't afford a lamb; instead, they offered the birds. The second ceremony was the redemption of the firstborn (Luke 2:23). In Exodus 13:2 we read: 'Consecrate to me all the firstborn: whatever is the first to open the womb among the Israelites, of human beings and animals, is mine.' Just as the firstborn male animals could be bought back, so too could the boys. According to Numbers 18:15–16 the child could be bought back by paying the priest the sum of five shekels.

Both of these ceremonies belong to a past era and no longer apply to Christians today. However, there are elements in the story of the presentation of Jesus that are of relevance. For instance, in the first place Mary and Joseph brought Jesus to the temple because they were a God-fearing couple who were determined to go God's way; they wanted God to be at the centre of their life together as a family, and in this respect they set us an example. Secondly, Mary and Joseph almost certainly brought Jesus to the temple because they wanted their child to be blessed. Presumably, Simeon, when he took the baby Jesus into his arms, not only praised God, but also blessed the child, using no doubt the words of the Aaronic blessing (Num. 6:24–26). But, thirdly, Simeon also 'blessed' Mary and Joseph (2:34). Here we have a reminder that not only the child, but also the parents, need God's blessing. It is no easy task bringing up children.

The interest of the story, however, does not lie in what Mary and Joseph did to Jesus, but in what Simeon said about Jesus. In particular, Simeon used three metaphors to speak about the impact Jesus would have on the world.

First of all, Simeon described Jesus as 'a light for revelation to the Gentiles and for glory to your people Israel' (2:32). Almost certainly, Simeon was drawing upon prophecies relating to the Servant Messiah contained in the second half of Isaiah, where God's servant is similarly called to be a light to the nations so that all the world might be saved (Isa. 42:1–6; 49:6). As he held the baby Jesus in his arms, Simeon realized that this child would dispel not only Israel's darkness, but the darkness of the world.

Secondly, Simeon likened Jesus to a rock. True, the actual word 'rock' does not appear, but the idea is certainly present. It is present when Simeon declares: 'This child is destined for the falling and the rising of many in Israel' (2:34). In the Old Testament the idea of a rock of stumbling appears a number of times: for instance, in Isaiah 8:14. However, Isaiah also likened God to a rock of salvation on which people could build securely (Isa. 28:16). In other words, the one and the same rock can lead to destruction and also to salvation. Simeon takes up this twofold concept: this baby will cause some to fall, but others to rise. A similar idea is found in Paul: to some the cross is a stumbling-block, but to others it is the means of salvation (1 Cor. 1:22–23). Or to put it another way, the light that dispels darkness, also creates shadows.

The third metaphor present is that of a sword. To Mary, Simeon said: 'a sword will pierce your own soul too' (2:35). Simeon, with Jesus in his arms, foresaw opposition. He will be 'a sign that will be opposed' (2:34); indeed, he foresaw that opposition would reach such a pitch that it would lead to death – a sword would pierce through his soul – and through yours 'too', Mary. Here we have a reminder of the cost of our salvation. It cost Jesus dearly; it cost Mary his mother dearly; and, of course, it cost God the Father dearly too.

A tribute to Simeon

I would have loved to preach at Simeon's funeral. There would have been so many good and positive things I could have said about him.

He was a man of faith, 'looking forward to the consolation of Israel' (2:25): that is, 'he was waiting for Israel to be saved' (GNB). It couldn't have been an easy wait; we don't know his exact age, but clearly he was an old man waiting to die. But he hadn't given up hope. He had kept the faith, when perhaps many might have given up. To his great delight, he discovered that the God in whom he had believed keeps his promises. No wonder he burst into a song of praise.

He was a man filled with the Holy Spirit. Three times in verses 25–27 we have a reference to the Spirit at work in his life. Simeon is a reminder that the Holy Spirit was active before Pentecost. But whereas before Pentecost the Spirit was active only in the lives of certain special people, from Pentecost onward the Spirit is given to all who put their trust in Jesus. Would that all the followers of Jesus had the spiritual wisdom of Simeon! He was a man gifted with insight and discernment!

He was a good man, 'righteous and devout' (2:25). That is, he had a good and positive relationship both with God and with his fellow Jews. The word 'righteous' describes his behaviour towards others; the word 'devout' describes his relationship towards God. In our terms, he had not simply a Sunday faith, but a Monday–Saturday faith. Would that all the followers of Jesus could be described as good people: people whose lives are consistent with their faith!

He was a blessing to parents and children alike, for he blessed both Mary and Joseph (2:34), as presumably also the baby Jesus (2:28). Would that could be said of all of God's people. Sadly, it's all too easy for older people to criticize young parents. It's all too easy too for older people not to know the names of children in the church, let alone to take an interest in them.

He pointed people to Jesus. His prayer (known as the Nunc Dimittis) pointed very clearly to Jesus as the Saviour of the world: In this respect Simeon challenges us all; but perhaps there is a particular challenge to the retired to share their faith with the many older people still searching for meaning and purpose, desperate for a faith that enables them to face up to death.

Yes, I would have liked to have preached at Simeon's funeral. There would have been so many positive things I could have said about him. God grant that when we die, we could be as positive about one another, as I have been about Simeon!

The aged Anna: a model of faith

According to most English versions, Anna was eighty-four years old. However, Anna might have been even older, for the underlying Greek is a little ambiguous and could be translated: 'she had been married for only seven years and been a widow eighty-four years'. If this latter translation is right, then she would have been just over 100. For in those days girls tended to get married around the time when they were twelve years old: add seven years of marriage and another eighty-four years and we get 103. No wonder Luke speaks of her being 'of a great age'!

At any time it is hard to lose one's life partner. But it must have been particularly hard to lose a husband after only seven years of marriage, particularly in a society where there was no social security and no widow's benefit. Life must have been very tough for Anna. However, her difficulties do not appear to have made Anna turn her back on God: if anything, they made her turn to God. Luke tells us that 'she never left the temple but worshipped there with fasting and prayer night and day' (2:37). We must beware of being overliteral: Luke is not trying to say that she never went home. Indeed, on that particular day when Mary and Joseph came with Jesus, it appears that she had just arrived in the temple. In other words, she did not actually live in the temple, but took every opportunity to be present at worship.

Some people, when tragedy strikes and a loved one dies, give up on God. They become hard and bitter, and blame God for the injustice they have suffered. The older they grow, the more resentful they become. They are not happy people to be around. But Anna was different. Instead of turning away from God, she turned to God; and in doing so she became a kinder, softer, more sympathetic woman. She lived up to her name: 'Grace'!

Then in her old age something special happened to Anna. She met Jesus. In her time Anna must have seen hundreds, if not thousands, of babies brought to the temple. But Anna, along with Simeon, was given the insight to realize that this was no ordinary baby. This was God's Messiah: the one for whom she and Simeon and other devout Jews had been waiting for years. At last the one who was going to set God's people free had arrived. For Anna, her last years were her best years. For it was then that she met the Saviour.

But Anna did not simply meet the Saviour. She went on to tell other people about the Saviour: Luke tells us that she spoke 'about the child to all who were looking for the redemption of Jerusalem' (2:38). Again, the English translation may well be misleading, for it could imply that she spoke only once to others about Jesus; whereas the Greek uses a past continuous (imperfect) tense: 'she kept speaking'. Anna provides us with quite a model of faith!

An overview: Jesus the revolutionary

A major feature of Luke's account of the birth of Jesus is the exemplary role played by women. Elizabeth, and not Zechariah, is the person of true faith: for while Zechariah is struck dumb because of his lack of faith (1:20), Elizabeth, 'filled with the Holy Spirit' (1:41), happily greets Mary as the 'mother of my Lord' (1:43). Mary, and not Joseph, comes across as the model disciple. For while Joseph stands in the shadows and plays no active part, Mary's response to Gabriel is one of obedient faith: 'Here am I, the servant of the Lord; let it be with me according to your word' (1:38). And while Simeon is simply content to see the Christ-child, it is left to Anna to tell others the news of the Saviour (2:38).

At a time when women had few, if any rights, and were generally treated as second-class citizens, the leading role of women in Luke's account is truly remarkable. In the Jewish world of Jesus' day women were very much inferior to men. In the Jewish Talmud we read such statements as: 'He that talks much with women brings evil upon himself and neglects the duy of the Law and at last will inherit Gehenna' (*Mish Aboth* 1:5); 'Every man who teaches his daughter Torah is as if he taught her promiscuity' (*Mish Sotah* 3:4); 'Let the words of the Torah be burned up, but let them not be delivered to women' (*Jer Sotah* 19a); and 'All we can expect of them [women] is that they bring up our children and keep us from sin' (*Bab Yebamoth* 63a). The Greeks and Romans were similarly dismissive of women and depicted women as

> basically ineducable and empty-headed; vengeful, dangerous and responsible for men's sins; mendacious, treacherous and unreliable; fickle; . . . incapable of moderation or spontaneous goodness; at their best in the dark; interested only in sex – unless they are with their own husbands, in which case they would rather talk. In short, women are one and all 'a set of vultures', the 'most beastly' of all the beasts on land or sea, and marriage is at best a necessary evil.[14]

How right Mary was to sing, 'He has brought down the powerful from their thrones, and lifted up the lowly' (Luke 1:52). In a way in

---

14. Charles Carlston, quoted by Richard N. Longenecker, *New Testament Social Ethics for Today* (Grand Rapids: Eerdmans, 1984), p. 72.

which she could not have dreamed, the coming of Jesus had set in train the most profound of all revolutions. So much so, that Paul could later write: 'There is no longer Jew or Greek, there is no longer slave or free, there is no longer male and female; for all of you are one in Christ Jesus' (Gal. 3:28). In Jesus divisions of race, social status and gender are overcome. In Jesus there is no room for prejudice or chauvinism, nor is there any place for a sense of inferiority or indeed superiority. The coming of Jesus has been truly revolutionary.

3 The Good News according to John

John paints the coming of Jesus in the boldest of colours. For whereas for Matthew and Luke the town of Bethlehem is the scene of Jesus' coming into the world, for John the universe is the stage. For this reason he dispenses with the stories of the shepherds and the wise men; there is no place in his Gospel for the angels or for the star. Instead, John depicts the cosmic significance of this baby, using categories of thought familiar to any thinking person of his day. 'The Word', declares John, 'became flesh' (John 1:14).

The term 'the Word' rings no bells for us today. But for John's contemporaries it was a term of enormous significance. It is no exaggeration to say that it was an 'international' term with connotations buried deep in the cultures of both the Eastern and Western world. The ancient Assyrians and Babylonians composed hymns about the Word of God. The Greeks and the Romans too had long speculated about the nature of the Word of God. For example, the philosopher Heraclitus in the sixth century BC described the Word as 'the omnipresent wisdom by which all things are guided' and regarded the Word as virtually equivalent to God. Similarly, the Jews were familiar with a figure whom they sometimes termed the

Wisdom of God, and at other times termed the Word of God. Philo, a Jewish contemporary of Jesus who lived in Alexandria, published book after book dealing with the Word of God. He stated that for the mass of people God is unknowable, but ordinary folk could know him in and through the Word.[1] Do we get the picture? Just as today people of every culture know that Levi's are a type of trousers, so then people of every culture knew that 'the Word' had something to do with God.

What does all this mean to us? The very internationalism of the term is a pointer to the fact that Jesus cannot be confined to any particular culture or group of people. Yes, Jesus came as a first-century Jew and lived among Jews. The feet of Jesus never walked on England's green and pleasant land – all that is a myth: they walked only on the dry and dusty roads of Palestine. And yet Jesus cannot be limited to one particular culture or group of people, nor can he be limited to a particular time within history. For Jesus is 'the Word', and as such has significance for all people of all time. He has significance for us too. For in Jesus, the Word of God, all our longings for God are met. For Jesus is God's own self-expression. As J. B. Phillips put it in his paraphrase: 'At the beginning God expressed himself. That personal expression, that word, was with God, and was God.'

Jesus is the universal Word (John 1:1–5)

In the beginning was the Word, and the Word was with God, and the Word was God. He was in the beginning with God. All things came into being through him, and without him not one thing came into being. What has come into being in him was life, and the life was the light for all people. The light shines in the darkness, and the darkness did not overcome it.

Jesus, the Word of God
John in this opening prologue to his Gospel says three crucial things about Jesus, the Word, in terms of his relationship to God.

---

1. For further background material see G. R. Beasley-Murray, *John*, Word Biblical Commentary 36 (Waco, Texas: Word, 1987), pp. 6–10.

First, he is beyond all time. 'In the beginning was the Word' (1:1a). Mark Stibbe comments: 'Most stories begin with a sense of "once upon a time", with a sense of a beginning somewhere in the past. John's story of Jesus begins with a sense of "once before time".'[2] In the beginning, before time ever was, the Word was! John's opening echoes the opening of the book of Genesis; but whereas Genesis refers to God's activity at the beginning of creation, here we learn of a being who existed before creation took place. Jesus does not belong to the created order: he was with the Father before time began. This means, therefore, that the Jesus whose birth we celebrate existed long before he took human form. At this point we begin to struggle to comprehend how one who was there before time began, who shared the very life of eternity with God, could become human. It was not that a normal child was somehow endowed with divinity, but rather that in a way which defies all human understanding 'the Word became flesh'. No new person began in Mary's womb; rather, the pre-existent Word came in human form. In the words of one theologian, Jesus was 'begotten outside time from the Father, without a mother. He was begotten in time from his mother, without a father.'[3]

It is at this point that reason has to give way to faith. We are dealing here with mystery. Alas, there are some who refuse to accept mystery, as if reason must be the final arbiter of truth. But surely, if we are dealing with God, it is only natural that his ways will be beyond our understanding and comprehension. The moment God and his ways are truly comprehensible, that moment he is no longer God, but rather a creation of our own imagination.

Something of the mystery of the incarnation was conveyed by Cardinal Basil Hume in a homily entitled 'A sense of wonder':

> None of us will ever be able to fathom completely the meaning of the incarnation. I often reflect that it is better to kneel humbly and devoutly at the crib and wonder prayerfully about the fact of Our Lord's birth. Better that than to try to understand fully with the power of our own minds the truths

---

2. Mark W. G. Stibbe, *John* (Sheffield: Sheffield Academic Press, 1993), p. 22.
3. Kallistos Ware.

of our faith . . . There is a pride of the mind which rejects what it cannot understand and denies what it cannot prove. How important it is to recognise that faith begins when reason can go no further. It is faith that enables us to see in the child in the crib, not just a child, but him of whom St John wrote: 'The Word was made flesh and dwelt amongst us'. Not to believe is a modern disease.[4]

Secondly, he is distinct from God: 'The Word was with God' (1:1b). God cannot simply be equated with Jesus. Alas, sometimes we confuse the persons of the Trinity. I sometimes hear people addressing God as Father and thanking him for dying on the cross. But God the Father did not die on the cross; Jesus the incarnate Son of God did. The truth is that Jesus is a distinct person within the Godhead.

The underlying Greek preposition (*pros*) translated in the NRSV as 'with God' means 'in the company of', 'in communion with', 'face to face'. It speaks of a personal relationship, as distinct from physical proximity. John is telling us that the Word eternally existed in a person-to-person relationship with God. Later John describes this relationship in terms of Father and Son. It is a relationship of love and intimacy.

What does this mean for us? It surely means that nobody can tell us what God is like, what God's love and heart and mind are like, as Jesus can. To take a simple human analogy: if we want to know what someone really thinks and feels about something, and if we are unable to approach the person ourselves, we do not go to someone who has known that person only a short time, but rather to someone who has known that person for many years. To say, therefore, that there never was a time when 'the Word was' not 'with God' is to say that Jesus knows all there is to know of God. Jesus is, therefore, the one person in all the universe who can reveal to us what God is like.

Thirdly, he is one with God: 'and the Word was God' (1:1c). Actually, in the original Greek the word order is the other way round: 'and God was the Word'! How can Jesus at one and the same time be 'with God' and be 'God'? The correspondence between the two

---

4. Basil Hume, *The Mystery of the Incarnation* (London: Darton, Longman & Todd, 1999), p. 24.

clauses is not quite as exact as it might appear. In the first clause, where John says 'the Word was with God', the Greek definite article is used of God, whereas in the second clause, 'and God was the Word', the definite article is absent. For this reason the Watch Tower translation of the Bible used by Jehovah's Witnesses reads: 'the Word was a god'. But John could never have meant that; like any good Jew and as the rest of his Gospel witnesses, he believed in one God, and one God alone. What John is saying is that the Word was 'God in his nature'. Or as the REB/NEB put it: 'and what God was, the Word was'. Had John used the definite article, then the impression might have been given that the Word was all there was in God, whereas in fact the Word was but part of the Godhead. The Word of God did not 'exhaust' the being of God. The Word of God shared in the life of the Godhead, and yet at the same time retained his own separate identity.

Here is a mystery, with which the finest minds have wrestled. John does not reflect philosophically on the Trinity, but simply bears witness to it as the eternal reality; he leaves it to later teachers to expound. In the words of the Nicene Creed, formulated in AD 325 and the church's first serious attempt to define its explanation of Jesus Christ: 'We believe in one Lord, Jesus Christ, the only Son of God, eternally begotten of the Father, God from God, Light from Light, true God from true God, begotten, not made, of one Being with the Father'. The truth, however, is that the relationship of Jesus to the Father defies all understanding. As one theologian rightly said: 'The fact is that in its central conviction the Church has been satisfied in its soul, although it has never achieved an explanation that has satisfied the mind.'[5]

Jesus is the Word, and yet no words can fully define his role. He is not, however, beyond our worship. The apostle Paul was right when he wrote to the Corinthians: 'Thanks be to God for his indescribable gift!' (2 Cor. 9:15).

Jesus is the Word of life
Jesus, the Word of God, is the Word of life: that is, he is the life-giving Word active both in creation and in re-creation.

---

5. John W. Carlton.

In the first place, he is active in creation, for he is the mediator of creation: 'All things came into being through him, and without him not one thing came into being' (1:3). There are no exceptions: the existence of absolutely all things came by the Word. The truth of this is expressed first positively ('all things came into being through him') and then negatively ('without him not one thing came into being'). Here again we are dealing with facts that are hard to comprehend. Until discoveries made in the 1920s, the Milky Way was thought to be the entire universe, but now we realize there are many billions of galaxies. What an amazing world we live in. How even more amazing its creator must be!

Incidentally, we should not confuse the fact of creation with the process. If we want to know how the world was made, then we should turn to the scientists. If we want to know who made the world, then we should turn to God. In this respect Albert Einstein once wrote of his famous 'relativity theory': 'I want to know how God created this world – I want to know his thoughts – the rest are details.'

It was through Jesus, the Word, that God created the world. We should notice that, strictly speaking, the Word is not the creator: he is the mediator of creation. John does not say that all thing were made 'by' him, but 'through him'. Ultimately, God alone is the source of all life. The apostle Paul expresses the same truth in 1 Corinthians 8:6: 'there is one God, the Father, from whom are all things and for whom we exist, and one Lord, Jesus Christ, through whom are all things and through whom we exist'. Creation was not the solitary work of the Father or of the Son: both were at work, and still are. What a challenging thought. For John is telling us that the ultimate explanation of the universe is not to be found in the formulas of physics, but in the person whom John calls the Word of God.

He is also saying that this is God's world, and that by implication everything that happens to this world is of interest to God. If this is so, then so-called 'green' issues are of importance to God.

That species are being exterminated, forests denuded, soil eroded, rivers and seas polluted and the ozone layer depleted, contradicts the creative action of our Lord Jesus Christ who called all things into being. Although affected by fallenness, they remain his personal handiwork. A lack of concern for our natural environment is a sign of a limited view of Christ, or of a spirituality which is more spiritual than Jesus and in need of balance and healing.[6]

John goes on to state that this life-giving Word is also the mediator of the new creation: 'In him was life, and the life was the light of all people' (1:4). The Word was not simply active in creation, but also in the new creation. Precisely because sin and death had invaded God's world, 'the Word became flesh' in order to bring us life. As Jesus said to the crowds: 'I came that they may have life, and have it abundantly' (John 10:10). As he said to his disciples: 'I am the way, and the truth, and the life. No one comes to the Father except through me' (John 14:6). In other words, without Jesus we may exist, but we do not truly live. Only in Jesus do we truly come alive.

How do we come alive? The message of John is that we need to believe. Towards the end of his Gospel he writes that he has written his account of Jesus 'so that you may come to believe . . . and that through believing you may have life in his name' (20:31).

It is surely this conviction that underlies all our Christmas activities. We want others to discover that in Jesus alone 'life' and 'light' are to be found. For Jesus alone is the true and living way to God.

The light of God

Have you ever experienced true darkness? Not the kind of darkness that we experience when night comes, for then there is the moon and there are the stars and we can still see. No, I have in mind pitch darkness. I remember once standing deep in the bowels of some caves. At a given moment the guide turned out the light, plunging us into sudden and total darkness. Not a flicker of light to be seen anywhere. Although we had been warned of what would happen, it was still a frightening experience. For where there is total darkness, we have no sense of direction: we feel totally lost.

John in his Gospel takes up the metaphor of darkness and uses it

---

6. Bruce Milne, *The Message of John* (Leicester: IVP, 1993), p. 41.

to describe the world in which we live. Against this frightening back-cloth John portrays Jesus as the light of the world. Although the theme of 'light' is found throughout John's Gospel (it is one of John's great keywords and occurs no fewer than twenty-one times), we shall focus on the prologue to discover what John meant when he described Jesus as 'the light of all people' (1:4).

In the first place, Jesus reveals the truth about God. Traditionally, this description of the Word being 'the light of all people' has been seen as a pointer to God's general revelation. John Calvin, for example, believed that these words refer 'to the common light of Nature'. John, it is argued, at this stage is talking not of the incarnate Jesus, but rather of the pre-existent Jesus. Jesus, the Living Word, by sharing in the creation of the world, points people to God. In this respect David J. Mansell's song 'Jesus is Lord' comes to mind: Creation's voice proclaims, and the whole universe declares the power and lordship of Jesus. The creation speaks of God. In the words of the psalmist:

> The heavens are telling the glory of God;
>   and the firmament proclaims his handiwork.
> Day to day pours forth speech,
>   and night to night declares knowledge. (Ps. 19:1–2)

It is precisely because of what the theologians term 'natural' or 'general' revelation, that men and women are religious. We only have to look around us to know that there is a greater power beyond ourselves.

But when John describes Jesus as 'the light of all people', he has far more in mind than a mere general pointing of men and women to God. For Jesus was not simply involved in the creation of the world: he came into our world. 'The Word became flesh and lived among us' (1:14), and in coming among us Jesus revealed the truth about God. John describes Jesus as 'the true light, which enlightens every-one, was coming into the world' (1:9). Jesus is 'the true light' over against other so-called 'lights', which are either 'false' or at best 'partial'. The Britain of today is a multicultural, multiracial and multi-faith society. As a result our children are no longer just taught about Christianity; they are also taught about all the other major world religions, about Hinduism, Buddhism, Islam and Judaism. I have no doubt that such teaching is good and proper. If we're going to live with people of different races, cultures and religions, it is important that we understand one another. However, in today's politically correct society the impression is sometimes given that all religions are of equal worth, that all religions lead to God. But this is not so. Jesus – and Jesus alone – is 'the true light'. He alone is the way to salvation.[7]

The reason why Jesus is 'the true light' is that he has come from God. Other religions are attempts by people to reach up to God. But in Jesus God has come to us. It is this thought that is behind John 1:18: 'No one has ever seen God. It is God the only Son, who is close to the Father's heart, who has made him known.'

How did Jesus reveal the truth about God? In part Jesus revealed the truth about God in his teaching. For instance, in the Sermon on the Mount, Jesus tells his disciples not to worry, for our heavenly Father knows our needs and will supply those needs when we seek first his kingdom and his righteousness (Matt. 6:25–34). Or in the Parable of the Prodigal Son, Jesus depicts God as the Waiting Father, waiting for the prodigal to return home (Luke 15:11–32). But, more importantly, Jesus has revealed the truth about God in his actions. It is in his coming into our world and above all in his dying on a cross that we see something of the depth of God's love for us and, indeed, for all people. As John was later to write in his first letter: 'God's love was revealed among us in this way: God sent his only Son into the world so that we might live through him. In this is love, not that we loved God but that he loved us and sent his Son to be the atoning sacrifice for our sins' (1 John 4:9–10).

But Jesus does not simply reveal the truth about God: he also reveals the truth about ourselves. So John writes: 'The light shines in the darkness' (1:5). When the light of Jesus breaks into our lives, we not only see God for who he is; we also see ourselves for what we are; and the result is not a happy picture. For whereas we see the love of God in all its brilliance, we also see our self-love, our

---

7. In the Old Testament, 'light' is often a symbol of salvation: see, for instance, Ps. 27:1; Isa. 49:6; 60:19–20.

self-centredness, in all its horrifying nastiness. John puts it this way: 'people loved darkness rather than light because their deeds were evil. For all who do evil hate the light and do not come to the light, so that their deeds may not be exposed' (3:19–20). The temptation is to apply these words just to non-Christians, to people who deliberately turn their back on Jesus and his claim on their lives. But are there not times when we, who profess to love the Lord Jesus, also prefer darkness to light? The fact is that the light of his love exposes the shabbiness of our own lives. In the light of Jesus even the best of what we offer to God is seen to be pretty grubby.

To those outside it may appear that we are serving God, but the truth is that all too often our motives are mixed. The great Scottish minister Alexander Whyte once said: 'If you knew my heart, you would spit in my face.' Hypocrisy abounds, not least in religious circles. We may kid others that we are good, but the light of Jesus exposes us for what we are. Sometimes we even kid ourselves that we are good. It is amazing how unaware people are of themselves and of their motives. But when we truly open up our lives to Jesus, his light reveals the cobwebs, the dirt, the muck that encrust our souls. It can be a painful experience to encounter Jesus. 'Go away from me, Lord,' said Peter on one occasion, 'for I am a sinful man!' (Luke 5:8). A certain Alcibiades used to say to his friend, the great Greek philosopher Socrates: 'Socrates, I hate you, for every time I meet you, you let me see what I am.'[8] What may have been true of Socrates, is even more true of Jesus. His light exposes us for what we are: sinners.

Thirdly, Jesus reveals the meaning of life: 'The light shines in the darkness' (1:5). It may well be that John intends here to have an echo of the creation story in Genesis 1. When God made the world, there was 'darkness', but 'Then God said, "Let there be light"; and there was light' (Gen. 1:3). In the creation story, the light is almost a synonym for the order that was brought out of the primeval chaos. Jesus, as the 'light of all people', brings order out of our chaos, in the

---

8. Quoted by William Barclay, *The Gospel of John*, I, Daily Study Bible, 2nd ed. (Edinburgh: St Andrew Press, 1956), p. 131.

sense that he gives meaning and purpose to a life that otherwise would appear to have neither.

English has an expression 'to be in the dark', and by that we mean 'not to not know what's happening, what's it all about'. Without Jesus, people are in the dark. Life has no meaning. In Samuel Beckett's play *Waiting for Godot*, the two main characters are two tramps who in utter boredom wait for Godot to turn up. They don't know who Godot is, and at the end of the play, when he's failed to appear, one tramp says to the other: 'Well, shall we go?' 'Yes, let's go,' replies the other. But the final stage direction says: 'They do not move.'[9] They don't move, because they don't know where to go. That sums up life for many. Life for many is lived in the dark. But 'the light shines in the darkness'. And where there is light, there is meaning, purpose, direction.

Fourthly, Jesus reveals the way to life, in the sense that he guides us on the way to life. Without following the light he sheds, we end up in disaster. The story is told of a man in the USA flying his single-engine plane towards a small country airport. It was late in the day, and before he could get the plane into position to land, dusk fell and he could not see the hazy field below. He had no lights on his plane and there was no-one on duty at the airfield below. He began circling, but the darkness deepened, and for two hours he flew that plane around and around, knowing that he would certainly crash when his fuel ran out. But then a 'miracle' occurred. Someone on the ground heard his engine and realized his plight. A man drove his car back and forth on the runway, to show where the airstrip was and then shone the headlights from the far end of the strip to guide the pilot to a safe landing. Jesus is the light and the way for our lives. Disaster lies in the darkness. Jesus said: 'I am the light of the world. Whoever follows me will never walk in darkness but will have the light of life' (John 8:12). Jesus, of course, did not have in mind the lights of an aerodrome, for that is a modern phenomenon. Nor did he have in mind the light of a lighthouse warning ships of the danger of rocks and guiding them safely into harbour, even though

---

9. Samuel Beckett, *Waiting for Godot: A Tragicomedy in Two Acts* (London: Faber & Faber, 1956).

lighthouses were known in the ancient world. No, he almost certainly had in mind the pillar of fire, which had gone before the children of Israel as they journeyed through the wilderness (see Exod. 13:17–22).

Jesus guides us through the desert of life. For the Jews this was a very meaningful picture, not just because of their history, but also because of their geography. Their country was bounded by the desert to the south, to the east and to the north. It was all too easy for ignorant travellers to leave the beaten track and die a lonely and awful death. 'I am the light of the world. Whoever follows me will never walk in darkness'. Without Jesus we lose our way, we go astray, but with Jesus we find the way to life.

We should note the ongoing nature of this following the light. There is more to the Christian life than simply making a decision to follow Christ: we have to keep following! Here we have a reminder that salvation is a process, and not just an event. As Christians we are followers of the way. We must always follow Jesus.

Finally, John reminds us that the light of Jesus has not been extinguished: 'The light shines in the darkness' (1:5). When John wrote his Gospel, at least thirty, if not fifty, years had elapsed since Jesus had died on the cross of Calvary. And yet John uses a present tense, rather than a past tense. This is all the more unexpected, since in the previous sentence he has used the past tense: 'What has come into being in him was life, and the life was the light of all people.' But all of a sudden he switches to the present: 'The light shines'. The light not only shone when Jesus was born in Bethlehem, when he went around Galilee doing good, and when he gave his life for us in Jerusalem. 'The light still shines' (J. B. Phillips); indeed, it continues to shine today. That is, Jesus continues to reveal the truth about God, the truth about ourselves, the meaning of life, the way to life. The gospel of Jesus is not just good news for a past generation; it is good news for ours too.

Light in the dark

When I see candles burning everywhere in church, many of them guttering in the draught, my mind goes to the song Elton John sang at Princess Diana's funeral: 'Candle in the wind'. There was a candle-like quality of life to Diana. In a dark and cold world she was for many a child, and for many an AIDS sufferer a flame of hope and love; and in a world strewn with landmines she became a flame of energy, fragile and yet strong enough to bring about change. But on Sunday 31 August 1997 that light was extinguished. And the hope and the love and the energy died with her. True, her memory will survive. For many years we in the UK shall as a nation remember Diana. And yet the time will come when she will fade from our collective memory. The light of her memory, let alone of her life, will be no more. But nearly two thousand years ago, into the bleakness of our suffering world, came a flame of love that no darkness could or ever will extinguish. In the words of John: 'The light shines in the darkness, and the darkness did not overcome it' (1:5).

As we have noticed, John uses a present tense, rather than a past tense: 'The light shines'. Nobody has been able to put out the light of Jesus. Cruel Herod laid his plans of genocide, but he could not put out the light. Weak Pilate ignored the demands of justice and condemned Jesus to die, but he could not put out the light. The Roman emperor Trajan sent thousands of Christians to their deaths in a bloodbath intended to do away with the church, but he could not put it out. The German philosopher Nietzsche created his superman, designed to stuff Jesus back into his grave, but he could not put it out. Today's postmodern generation devise their new subjective moralities, but they cannot put out the light. 'The light shines in the darkness, and the darkness did not overcome it.' Or as another version puts it (Peterson, *The Message*): 'The Life-Light blazed out of the darkness; the darkness couldn't put it out.' Here is good news indeed for a world that lives in darkness. The light shines.

It is good news, precisely because life without God is dark. Yes, without God life has no real direction or purpose. Without God we are lost. Without God there is no meaning, no purpose, only darkness. This was the sad experience of a young teenage girl, who looked like an old woman, and who had just given birth to a baby already hooked on drugs. To a nurse who was trying to help her she said: 'Don't talk to me about love and meaning. Life is just a long black tunnel. You go in it and never find your way out.'

The good news is that there is a way out of the tunnel. For Jesus, the light of the world has come. Jesus, who said: 'I am the light of the world. Whoever follows me will never walk in darkness but will have the light of life' (John 8:12). Jesus, of whom Charles Wesley wrote in his carol, 'Hark! The herald angels sing':

> Light and life to all he brings
> risen with healing in his wings.

So don't let us stay in the dark. Let us come into the light.

A witness to the light (John 1:6–8)

There was a man sent from God, whose name was John. He came as a witness to testify to the light, so that all might believe through him. He himself was not the light, but he came to testify to the light.

Traditionally, the third Sunday of Advent has been termed 'Ministry Sunday'. It is on this Sunday that the church has prayed for its ministers. The reason for this focus on Christian ministry is that the Gospel reading for the day always focuses on the person of John the Baptist, the one whom God sent to prepare the way for the coming ministry of Jesus. Along with the rest of the Christian church, we too shall focus on John the Baptist. But in doing so we shall discover that he offers not simply a model to ministers, but a model to us all.

'There was a man sent from God, whose name was John' (1:6). That's all the background information that the Fourth Gospel gives about John the Baptist. We know, however, from Luke that John was the only son of an elderly couple, the priest Zechariah and his wife Elizabeth. What's more, Luke tells us that he was the cousin of Jesus, for Elizabeth was related to Mary, the mother of Jesus. But we know little more about John than that. Some have speculated that Zechariah and Elizabeth died when John was quite young; and that he was subsequently looked after by members of the Dead Sea Community and that it was there at Qumran that he received his initial theological training. We know that this Dead Sea Community used to look after orphans. We also know that they were very much into baptizing. And it was in the vicinity of Qumran that John began his ministry. But whether or not he was ever actually a member of the community, we don't know. It's mere speculation.

John put Jesus first, and so too should we

When we turn to the Bible, we find its pages abound with the names of people who were famous because they were associated with even more important personalities. For example, Aaron was famous because of his association with Moses; Caleb was famous because of his association with Joshua; Jonathan was famous because of his association with David; and Barnabas was famous because of his association with Paul. But the greatest of all these 'second strings' was John the Baptist. Indeed, on one occasion Jesus himself said: 'Truly I tell you, among those born of women no one has arisen greater than John the Baptist' (Matt. 11:11). Yet for all his greatness, he never quite reached the top – for his task was to point to Jesus. John has therefore been described as the 'patron saint of all silver medallists'.

But he was more than a patron saint to the runners-up; he offers a model of sainthood to us all, in the sense that he always put Jesus first. Have you ever noticed that every reference to John the Baptist in the Fourth Gospel is a reference of depreciation: indeed, for the most part of self-depreciation? For example, John says to the priests and Levites sent from Jerusalem: 'I am not the Messiah' (1:20); similarly, to his disciples John again says, 'I am not the Messiah' (3:28), and instead he likens himself to the 'the friend of the bridegroom' (3:29), in our terms, the 'best man'. Here in the prologue to John's Gospel we read: 'He himself was not the light, but he came to testify to the light' (1:8).

It seems that there were certain people around who were so fascinated by John that they gave him a higher place than he ought to have had. They became his disciples rather than the disciples of Jesus. What's more, this was not just a local Palestinian phenomenon. For example, when Paul went to preach at Ephesus, he met there a group of disciples of John the Baptist (Acts 19:1–7). John, however, had no desire to become a cult figure. When the emissaries of the Pharisees asked him who he was, if he was not the Messiah or some other Messianic figure, he replied: 'I baptize with water. Among you stands one you do not know, the one who is coming after me; I am not worthy to untie the thong of his sandal' (1:26–27). As far as John was concerned, he had but a minor role in God's plan of salvation. A little later he said of Jesus: 'He must increase, but I must decrease' (3:30).

John was content to play 'second fiddle'. That in itself is unremarkable: there are plenty of people who are quite happy to take second place. But what is remarkable is that John was prepared to take second place, after he had gathered a considerable following. Yes, we may talk of John as being the 'patron saint of silver medallists', but in fact he was at one stage of his life an incredibly successful preacher. Both Matthew and Luke tell us that crowds of people flocked to hear him (Matt. 3:5; Luke 3:7). What's more, his preaching appealed to all classes and types of people: at the one end of the scale there were tax-collectors and soldiers, neither of which profession was known for its religiosity; while at the other end of the scale there were the upper-crust Sadducees and the theologically minded Pharisees. To cap it all, many responded to his preaching and were baptized by him in the river Jordan, confessing their sins. What more could a preacher want? Yet for all his success, he was happy to move over from the centre and take second place to Jesus. Indeed, we discover that when the crowds began to switch their attention to Jesus, John – far from being envious or bitter – actually rejoiced in what was happening. 'He must increase, but I must decrease' (3:30).

The more I reflect on these words, the more saintly a figure John becomes. John had given up everything to be a preacher. Comfort, ease, security, human love and family life; all these he had given up to follow his calling. And now the crowds were leaving him to follow Jesus. What's more, it was not just the crowds, but some of his disciples, even some of his closest friends like Andrew and John, were leaving him for Jesus. You would have thought that John would have been hurt. It would in fact have been understandable had John begrudged Jesus every recruit, had John even hated Jesus. It might not have been right, but we could have understood had John gone around belittling his rival's achievements.

But we read that when John was told that everyone was leaving him and going to Jesus instead, he replied: 'The friend of the bridegroom . . . rejoices greatly at the bridegroom's voice. For this reason my joy has been fulfilled' (3:29). John was content to be the frame, and to allow Jesus to be the painting. John set aside whatever personal ambition he might have had and put Jesus first. In so doing he provides a model for us, for we too should put Jesus first.

When it comes to our jobs, who comes first: Jesus or us? In some jobs promotion may perhaps be fairly automatic: provided people don't blot their copy book, they can't help but begin to climb the greasy ladder. But there comes a stage when perhaps the field begins to thin out and the real race is on. At this stage it is perhaps necessary to decide if one is going to sell one's soul to the company for the sake of getting on the next rung of the ladder. Indeed, there are times when all kinds of unethical wire-pulling may appear to be necessary to come out on top. At times like this, who comes first? Jesus or self?

John told others of Jesus, and so too should we

John the Baptist came to prepare the way for the coming of Jesus. In the words of the prologue, John 'came as a witness to testify to the light, so that all might believe through him' (1:7). When people asked him who he was, he answered by quoting the prophet Isaiah: 'I am the voice of one crying out in the wilderness, "Make straight the way of the Lord"' (1:23). He was the herald announcing the coming of the King of kings. His task was to call people to get ready for the coming of God's Messiah.

To appreciate the metaphor we have to remember that roads in the East were not strips of asphalt and tarmac: they were dirt tracks. When the emperor visited one of his far-flung provinces, the roads were smoothed and straightened out. Indeed, this didn't just happen in the East. I remember it happening in the Congo when President Mobutu was about to visit where we were living: the rutted dirt roads were scraped flat. It is against this background that we need to hear the cry 'Make straight the way of the Lord!' But the road that John had in mind was no ordinary road: he was thinking of people's lives that needed to be straightened out, of hearts that needed to be put right with God. John therefore called the people of his day to repentance: to turn from going their own selfish way and instead begin to go God's way.

One day, as John the Baptist was preaching, Jesus came to listen. When John had finished, Jesus stepped forward and asked to be baptized. Together they went down into the muddy waters of the Jordan. Suddenly, as John was hip deep in the river, something happened. It felt as if heaven had split open and John realized in one transforming moment something he had never known before: 'Here is the Lamb of God, who takes away the sin of the world!' (1:29). Here is the one for whom I have been preparing; here is 'the Lamb of

God'. This phrase, strange to us, was pregnant with meaning for any Jew. For to them a lamb symbolized freedom; it brought to mind the Passover lambs killed the night before Moses led the people of God on the greatest freedom march the world has ever known (see Exod. 12). To speak of Jesus as the Lamb of God was to speak of Jesus as the one who sets us free. How God was going to free his people, John could have had little idea. But we, who live on the other side of the cross and resurrection, know: for Jesus, the Lamb of God, gave his life that we might be free: free from sin and judgment of sin, free even from death and its sting.

So from preaching about repentance, John now turned to speak of Jesus. He told people that this 'Lamb of God' was the 'Son of God' (1:34). Or, in the words of the prologue: 'He came as a witness to testify to the light, so that all might believe through him' (1:7).

And what was true of John should be true of us too. We too should tell people about the light of the gospel of Jesus Christ, which brightens the life of all. John was a 'witness'. That very word 'witness' is actually a calling that belongs to every Christian. For Jesus, shortly before he ascended to his Father, said to his disciples: 'You will be my witnesses in Jerusalem, in all Judea and Samaria, and to the ends of the earth' (Acts 1:8). It is not just ministers who are to tell others of Jesus. Every Christian has a duty to tell others of Jesus too. Sharing the faith and telling others of Jesus is not a task for the gifted few, but is the duty of us all.

At times it is not easy sharing our faith. It is not without significance that the Greek word for 'witness' (*martys*) is the word from which we get our English word 'martyr'. Witnessing can be costly: in the case of John the Baptist it cost him his head. But there are times when it is easier to be a witness. Christmas is one of those times. Many people like hearing the traditional Christmas readings and singing familiar carols. So let's capitalize upon that and tell them the difference that Jesus has made to our lives.

Good news is for telling (John 1:10–13)

He was in the world, and the world came into being through him; yet the world did not know him. He came to what was his own, and his own people did not accept him. But to all who received him, who believed in his name, he gave power to become children of God, who were born, not of blood or of the will of the flesh or of the will of man, but of God.

This is God's world

Like most men, I don't easily drool over a baby and utter sweet nothings. Again, like most men, I don't become broody the moment I hold a baby in my arms. And yet every time I visit a newborn child I am overcome by a deep sense of wonder. I am overawed by the realization that the birth of a child is a miracle. Yes, I know that sometimes abnormalities do occur. Some children are born only to die, whereas others survive but live a life gravely limited by their disability. I would not wish to minimize the heartache caused by such births. But the fact is that the vast majority of children are born healthy and free of defects. All this is for me a miracle, a miracle brought about by God himself.

But it is not simply the birth-process that has a touch of God about it. The very world in which we live is a demonstration of the miraculous. According to the wisdom of the ancients there were seven wonders of the world. But surely they were wrong: there are countless wonders. The more I learn about the world in which we live, the more I marvel. True, from a scientific perspective the universe can perhaps be reduced to a set of complex laws, but how did those laws of nature come into being in the first place? Scientists today may speak of randomness and chance playing a role in the great evolutionary process, but how come we live in a resulting world of order, a world of order indeed in which scientists are able to discover patterns of being? The answer is that this is God's world. The more we know about it, the more awesome God appears.

Sadly, not everybody recognizes that this is indeed God's world. Some seem to think that the world just came into being by accident. I cannot see what logical reason there is for such a conclusion. To believe that this world came about by accident is about as logical as believing that the Oxford English Dictionary came about as a result of an explosion in a printing works. We may not believe in a literal seven-day creation, but the basic truth underlying Genesis 1 still remains true: 'In the beginning God created the heavens and the earth . . .'

It is precisely because this is God's world that the world's failure to recognize Jesus for who he is becomes so tragic. In the words of John's Gospel: 'He was in the world, and the world came into being through him: yet the world did not know him' (1:10). In John's day most people failed to see Jesus for who he was. And what was true then still remains true today. How tragic. In some ways the reaction of the world to Jesus is a bit like a concert audience rapturously applauding the performance of some immensely moving symphony or concerto, and yet refusing to give any credit to the composer as he comes on stage to take a bow. For this is God's world; and, along with his Father and the Spirit, Jesus had a hand, as it were, in creating the universe in which we live.

Yes, Jesus was no ordinary man. He was – and is – the Son of God. In a way that defies the imagination and the understanding, Jesus in his divine nature pre-existed as the Son of God, enjoying from eternity a relationship with the Father. As John says at the very opening of his Gospel, 'In the beginning was the Word, and the Word was with God, and the Word was God. He was in the beginning with God. All things came into being through him, and without him not one thing came into being' (John 1:1–3).

What an incredible statement! Interestingly, it is a statement that we find repeated in various other strands of the New Testament. To give but three examples: in 1 Corinthians 8:6 Paul wrote: 'there is one God, the Father, from whom are all things and for whom we exist, and one Lord, Jesus Christ, through whom are all things and through whom we exist'. In the Christ hymn of Colossians 1 we read: 'all things have been created through him and for him' (Col. 1:16). The very first sentence of the letter to the Hebrews describes Jesus as 'the one through whom he [God] also created the worlds' (Heb. 1:2).

Part of the sharing of the faith involves pointing out to our children that this is God's world. What's more, precisely because of Jesus' involvement, we can go on to say that this is a world that is suffused with love, the kind of love we find expressed in Jesus; this is a world in which we find only true meaning and fulfilment as we discover the God who has made himself known in Jesus. Yes, it is a wonderful world that God has made.

This is God's Son

It is not enough to point to the God who made the world. We need to point to the God who sent his Son. We need to point our friends to Jesus and say: 'This is God's Son.'

Sadly, not only did the world in general fail to recognize Jesus, many religious people also failed to accept him for who he was. 'He came to what was his own, and his own people did not accept him' (1:11).

When Jesus, God's Living Word, entered this world, he came to a particular country and to a particular people. He did not come to Rome or to Greece, nor to Egypt nor to any of the great Eastern empires. He came to Israel, to the land of the Jews. He came, says John, to 'his own people'. In the Old Testament, Palestine, the land of Israel, is repeatedly called 'the holy land' or 'the LORD's land' (see Zech. 2:12; Hos. 9:3; Jer. 2:7; 16:18; Lev. 25:23). Similarly the Jewish nation is repeatedly described as God's 'chosen' or 'special people' (see Exod. 19:5; Deut. 7:6). In a way that was not true of any other nation they had a special relationship with God. It was to the Lord's land, to the Lord's people, that Jesus came.

When, therefore, Jesus came to this land and to this people, he ought to have been welcomed with open arms. He should have been acclaimed as king. For they were a religious people. They were looking for God to send them a Messiah, a Saviour. But, as it was, Jesus was despised, he was rejected, and he ended up dying a premature death on a cross outside the holy city. What a tragedy. 'He came to . . . his own, and his own people did not accept him.' With the exception of a handful of disciples, the religious people of Jesus' day failed to receive Jesus as the one whom God had sent to be their Saviour. Sadly, that tragedy has been repeated many times over, in the sense that many people have thought themselves to be religious, and yet have missed out on the heart of true religion. They have believed in God, but have failed to receive God's greatest gift, the gift of his Son.

A survey in 2000, prepared for the BBC series of programmes entitled *The Soul of Britain*, revealed a majority still believed in God (62%), Jesus (62%), heaven (52%), life after death (51%), but more believed in a soul (69%) and sin (71%). A minority believed in hell (28%) and reincarnation (25%).[10]

---

10. *UK Christian Handbook Religious Trends 3* (London: Christian Research; Carlisle: Paternoster, 2001), 5.14.

Perhaps this is why still 50% of all babies born in the UK are baptized. Although less than 12% of the population of the UK claims membership of a Christian church in any active sense, many more people are still religious. People may no longer belong to a church, but they do still believe in God. But it is not enough simply to 'believe' in God. John here in his Gospel points out that we need to 'accept' Jesus. 'He came to what was his own, but his own people did not accept him'; they did not accept him in the sense that they did not welcome him into their hearts and their lives as their Saviour and their Lord.

Unfortunately, this need to receive Jesus has become unclear in the minds of many people, even religious people. It could be argued that the conversion of the emperor Constantine in AD 312 had disastrous consequences. For with his conversion the Roman Empire became 'Christian' and as a result the edges of faith became blurred and citizenship was confused with Christian faith. Tragically, this confusion has been with us ever since. We see it time and again when, for instance, most English people list themselves as 'C of E', even though it may have been years since they have darkened the door of a church for Sunday worship. But that's a farce. The fact is that it is only those who have accepted Jesus into their lives who can be termed 'Christians'. It is not enough to be born into a Christian home. Even going to church and observing the Golden Rule are not enough. We have to 'receive' the Lord Jesus into our hearts and lives.

This is my saviour

At some point faith needs to be personalized. John makes this clear when he writes: 'But to all who received him, who believed in his name, he gave power to become children of God, who were born, not of blood or of the will of the flesh or of the will of man, but of God' (1:12–13).

What does it mean to 'receive' the Lord Jesus? John says it means to 'believe in' him. That is, believing in Jesus is more than an intellectual activity, important as this is. It involves an activity of the will too. It involves 'putting our trust in' the Lord Jesus (see REB). The difference between believing and trusting is well illustrated in the story of Charles Blondin, a tightrope walker, who on one fine June day in 1858 crossed the Niagara Falls by walking 1,100 feet along a tightrope stretched from the American side of the falls to the Canadian side. On arriving at the Canadian side Blondin turned and issued a challenge to the watching crowd. He said he wanted to recross the falls with a man on his back. 'Do you believe I am able to carry you across?' he asked one in the audience. 'I certainly do,' replied the man. 'Then will you let me do it?' Blondin asked. 'Not on your life!' came the quick reply. He believed, but he did not trust.

C. S. Lewis once wrote:

> You never know how much you really believe anything until its truth or falsehood becomes a matter of life and death to you. It is easy to say you believe a rope to be strong and sound as long as you are merely using it to cord a box. But suppose you had to hang by that rope over a precipice. Wouldn't you then first discover how much you really trusted it?[11]

When it comes to believing in Jesus, of course, it really does involve a matter of life and death. In this respect the Blondin story is unhelpful. For Blondin was involved in a stunt, whereas Jesus is in the deadly serious business of salvation.

The salvation that Jesus has to offer is best expressed in some words we find a little further on in John's Gospel. There in John 3:16 we read: 'God so loved the world that he gave his only Son, so that everyone who believes in him may not perish but may have eternal life.' This is what it means to be a child of God: to be a child of God is to share in the life of God, a life that has no end. But in order to share in that life, in order to become a child of God, we have first to 'believe in' the Son, whom God sent into the world to live and die for us. We have first to put our trust in the crucified and risen Lord Jesus if he would be our Saviour. This is the good news we have to tell.

The Word became flesh (John 1:14–18)

And the Word became flesh and lived among us, and we have seen his glory, the glory as of a father's only son, full of grace and truth . . . From his

---

11. C. S. Lewis, *A Grief Observed* (London: Faber & Faber, 1961), p. 21.

*fullness we have all received, grace upon grace. The law indeed was given
through Moses; grace and truth came through Jesus Christ. No one has ever
seen God. It is God the only Son, who is close to the Father's heart, who had
made him known.*

'And the Word became flesh!' This is the staggering message we have
to proclaim Christmas after Christmas. In the words of Dorothy
Sayers, who created the character of Lord Peter Wimsey: 'From the
beginning of time until now it is the only thing which has ever really
happened . . . We may call this doctrine exhilarating or we may call it
devastating, we may call it revelation or we may call it rubbish . . .
but if we call it dull then what in heaven's name is worthy to be
called exciting?'[12]

At the time when John was writing his Gospel there was much
speculation by Greek philosophers about the so-called *Logos*, the
Word of God. There was much talk of the *Logos*, the Word, being
active in creation. But nowhere and at no time did those philosophers ever speak of the Word becoming flesh. That would have
been unthinkable. No Greek philosopher could ever have conceived of the Word of God taking human form. As far as the
Greeks were concerned the body was evil; they used to describe
the body as a prison house in which the soul was shackled, a tomb
in which the spirit was confined. 'The Word became flesh': 'Never!
You must be joking!'

So staggeringly new and unheard of was this conception of God
in human form, that there were some in the early church who
refused to believed the Word became flesh. Instead, they affirmed
that Jesus only *seemed* to be a man; in actual fact he was not. Such
people we call 'docetists'; the word is derived from a Greek word
that means 'to seem to be'. The docetists argued that the body of
Jesus was not real. Jesus did not really feel hunger and tiredness; he
did not really experience sorrow and pain. Indeed, they went on to
say that he did not really die on a cross: he just appeared to die.
These docetists proved quite a troublesome lot, so much so that in
his first letter John wrote: 'By this you know the Spirit of God: every

---

12. Dorothy Sayers, *Creed or Chaos?* (London: Harcourt, Brace, 1949), pp. 5, 7.

spirit that confesses that Jesus Christ has come in the flesh is from God, and every spirit that does not confess Jesus is not from God' (1 John 4:2–3). That is, one of the tests of whether or not a person is a Christian is whether or not they believe that God actually became one of us in the person of Jesus Christ. John was no docetist. He had a full-blooded belief in the incarnation. 'The Word became flesh'. God has come among us.

The wonder of Christmas

For some, Christmas is but a fairy tale. A. N. Wilson, for instance, tells of how he visited a cave where it was alleged Mary sat down to suckle the baby Jesus on the journey to Egypt, and how he was offered chalk-dust from the walls of the cave, which supposedly had formed from drops of Mary's milk. He then lumps this legend together with the biblical accounts of the birth of Jesus and calls the lot 'rubbish'.[13] But that's not fair! There is a world of a difference between the Gospels' restrained accounts of the birth of Jesus and later legendary developments.

However, the wonder of Christmas is not found in the stories of the shepherds and the wise men, with their angels and the star; it is found in John's statement that 'the Word became flesh and lived among us'. God the Son, who was with the Father before time began, has, without ceasing for a moment to be divine, become an authentic human person. Here is what C. S. Lewis rightly termed 'The Grand Miracle';[14] or what the leader of *The Times* in the run-up to Christmas 1993 described as 'the shocking centre of Christian faith, which dares to claim that in the fragility and contingency of a single human life the Creator knew his creation from the inside'.

The Canadian preacher Leonard Griffith once sought to explain the incarnation by telling a story about a Hindu who could not believe that the Infinite God would ever wish to become one of us.[15] One day he came across a colony of ants. He became interested in

---

13. A. N. Wilson, *Jesus* (London: HarperCollins Flamingo, 1993), p. 82.

14. C. S. Lewis, *Miracles* (London: Collins Fontana, 1960), pp. 112–135.

15. Leonard Griffith, *Barriers to Christian Belief* (London: Hodder & Stoughton, 2nd ed., 1967), pp. 93–94.

them, and as he bent over, his shadow fell across the ant hill. Immediately there was confusion among the insects: workers dropped their burdens, warrior ants came to defend their hill, and panic reigned. As the Hindu drew back, the sun fell again on the ant hill and order was gradually restored. But as he bent over it again, pain reappeared. Idly he began to wonder how he could bridge the gap between himself and the insects to show the ants that his drawing near indicated nothing but sympathy and interest. Then he realized that the only way in which this would be possible would be if he were somehow to become an ant himself, accepting the risks and terrors of life in the sand and grass. Only then could he communicate to the ants the intentions of his human heart. Suddenly he began to understand the meaning of the incarnation! 'The Word became flesh'. Here is indeed cause for wonder.

But the wonder continues. For the Word did not become flesh for a moment; he became flesh for a lifetime. 'The Word lived among us': literally, he 'camped among us', he 'pitched his tent among us'. The underlying Greek verb calls to mind the presence of God in the tabernacle or 'tent of meeting' (see Exod. 40:34). As God lived among his people then, so in Jesus he came and lived among us. True, his stay was limited, but no less real. Furthermore, in living among us he came and entered our experience. Unlike the docetists, who claimed that Jesus only appeared to be man, Jesus really could feel hunger and weariness, sorrow and pain. To quote *The Times* leader again, 'God comes into the muck and the mire. Part of the carnality of the incarnation is that God comes into the carnage.' Jesus entered our experience to the full. There is nothing he does not know or understand. Here too is cause for wonder.

The sense of wonder intensifies as we look at the end of the story and see that the incarnation but marked the beginning of an even more downward path to the cross. For the coming of God in the flesh cannot of itself save; the death of the God-Man was also required. In the words of Anselm, the eleventh-century theologian: 'Since no one save God can make satisfaction for our sins, and no one save man ought to make it, it is necessary for a God-man to make it.'[16] John 1:14

---

16. Anselm, *Why God Became Man* (Philadelphia: Westminster Press, 1956), p. 151.

needs to be read together with John 3:16. Jesus came to save us from our sin; he came that we might have eternal life.

It has been said that 'Every man has a right to his own opinion, but no man has a right to be wrong in his facts.'[17] In a similar vein Bertrand Russell declared:

> Aristotle could have avoided the mistake of thinking that women have fewer teeth than men by the simple device of asking Mrs Aristotle to keep her mouth open while he counted. He didn't do so, because he thought he knew. Thinking you know when you don't, is a fatal mistake to which we all are prone.[18]

What is true generally, is true in particular of the Christmas story. We need to face up to the fact that it is no fairy story, but that God really has come to us in Jesus. To fail to see the wonder of God coming to our rescue would indeed be 'a fatal mistake'.

Jesus became one with us

In the Festival of Nine Lessons and Carols held at King's College, Cambridge, the final lesson is always John 1:1–14. Here we come to the climax and central mystery of the Christmas story: 'the Word became flesh', Jesus became one with us.

In so doing, Jesus shared in the limitations of our living. The mind boggles that Jesus, God's Son, should limit himself to time and space; that the one who was involved in the very creation of the world should become one of us and take human form. In the words of C. S. Lewis: 'The Eternal Being, who knows everything and who created the whole universe, became not only a man but (before that) a baby, and before that a *foetus* inside a Woman's body. If you want to get the hang of it, think how you would like to become a slug or a crab.'[19] As Charles Wesley put it in one of his

---

17. Quoted by Anthony P. Castle, *More Quotes and Anecdotes* (Bury St Edmunds: Kevin Mayhew, 1997), p. 405.

18. Quoted by Robert Andrews (ed.), *Collins Thematic Dictionary of Quotations* (London: HarperCollins, 2nd ed., 1992), p. 234.

19. C. S. Lewis, *Mere Christianity* (London: Collins Fontana, 1955), p. 151.

hymns: 'Our God contracted to a span, Incomprehensibly made man'.[20]

In becoming one with us, Jesus undoubtedly shared in the joy of our living. As the life-giving Word, he surely was 'the life and soul' of every party. Unlike some Christians, Jesus was no life-denying wimp; rather, his life must have been characterized by a bubbling over of creativity and energy. As the one who had come that we might 'have life, and have it abundantly' (John 10:10), he must have lived life to the full. Jesus knew what it was like to enjoy life. We have no reason to think that he didn't enjoy himself at the wedding in Cana. This was his Father's world; he knew that his father had given him all good things to enjoy. Jesus was no world-denying ascetic.

But, in becoming one with us, Jesus also shared in the pain of our living. He knew what it was like to suffer. Jesus wasn't spared some of the harsher realities of life. 'The Word was made flesh', declares John. The very term 'flesh' reminds us of his frailty. Flesh is nervous, sensitive tissue that can easily be seared, bruised or battered by pain. Think of the terrible walk along the road we call the Via Dolorosa. Jesus knew what it was like to feel pain: the crown of thorns, the weight of the cross, the weals on his back from the lashings meted out to him. But Jesus didn't simply take on a human body. He also took on a human psyche, capable of feeling all the emotions we feel. He experienced not only the physical pain of the nails, but also the emotional pain of love spurned and rejected. The betrayal of Judas and the denial of Peter must have hurt him, for he was one with us.

Yes Jesus, in becoming one with us, shared our humanity to the full. In the words of Martin Luther: 'He ate, drank, slept, walked: was weary, sorrowful, rejoicing; he wept and he laughed; he knew hunger and thirst and sweat; he talked, he toiled, he prayed . . . so that there was no difference between him and other men, save only

---

20. From the hymn   Let earth and heaven combine,
                     Angels and men agree
                     To praise in songs divine
                     The incarnate Deity,
                     Our God contracted to a span,
                     Incomprehensibly made man.

this, that he was God and had no sin.'[21] And yet, the wonder of the gospel is that Jesus went further than simply sharing our humanity: he shared in our sinfulness. As Paul once put it: 'For our sake he made him to be sin who knew no sin, so that in him we might become the righteousness of God' (2 Cor. 5:21). Here we encounter further mystery. All the theological tomes in the world will never explain how Jesus could take sin, past, present and future upon himself. How could he take our sin upon himself, when we had yet to be born, yet alone to commit sin? And yet that is the wonder of the cross: that there one man died for all.

I don't understand. None of us understands. But then there are many things that most of us do not understand, but nonetheless we benefit from them. The fact, for instance, that we cannot all explain in any coherent form how television works does not stop us from benefiting from having a television. Likewise, we may benefit from the death of Christ, even although we may not understand. For it is not understanding, but simple faith that is called for. As John in his opening prologue puts it: 'But to all who received him, who believed in his name, he gave power to become children of God' (John 1:12).

God's word of love
One summer night a young mother tucked her small daughter into bed, while outside lightening flashed and thunder shook the house. After finally getting her daughter settled, the mother went downstairs and tried to read a book, but the storm kept up. Her daughter lay in bed as long as she could, but finally she jumped out of bed, ran downstairs and threw herself into her mother's arms. 'Mummy, I'm afraid,' she said. Her mother held and comforted her, and then the two of them walked upstairs. The mother went back downstairs. But five minutes later the little girl stood at the foot of the stairs: 'Mummy, I'm still afraid.' Her mother replied: 'Darling, I've told you that you have to get your sleep. You're perfectly safe. God loves you and he'll take care of you.' Her daughter replied: 'I know that God

---

21. Quoted by Norman Anderson, *The Mystery of the Incarnation* (London: Hodder & Stoughton, 1978), p. 56.

loves me. But Mummy, when it's thundering and lightning outside, I want someone with skin on to love me.'

The good news of Christmas is that someone with skin on has come to love us. When the storm roars about us and the lightning flashes, we need not be afraid: God has come to us, 'with skin on' as it were. Let us recall the prologue to John's Gospel: 'In the beginning was the Word, and the Word was with God, and the Word was God . . . And the Word became flesh and lived among us' (1:1, 14). In Jesus God has spoken a word of love. Indeed, more than merely spoken. For in Jesus God took three-dimensional form; he took an undiluted dose of humanity. In Jesus divine love took human form. Or in the words of the story about the little girl, we see God's love with skin on.

It is this that we celebrate at Christmas: God is love. Frederic Myers, a distinguished Victorian man of letters, was once asked: 'Suppose you could put one question to the Sphinx, with the certainty of getting an infallible answer, what would you ask?' Without a moment's hesitation he replied: 'I would ask, "Is the universe friendly?"' That cry represents the unspoken longing of countless hearts today. Is creation penetrated by a controlling purpose of good? Or is the world in which we live simply 'red in tooth and claw': where only the fittest of the species survive, where the weak and the vulnerable simply go to the wall? If there indeed is a God, does he love and care for us?

God does love us – he loves you and me; he has loved us with an everlasting love in Jesus. He has declared his love for us in the person of his Son, Jesus, the Word. In the first place God has declared his love for us in the birth of Jesus. In the words of John in his first letter: 'God's love was revealed among us in this way: God sent his only Son into the world' (1 John 4:9). This is mind-boggling stuff. It is mind-boggling not so much in terms of the mechanics, but in terms of the motivation. Whatever would possess the Lord of glory to empty himself of all that was rightfully his and become one of us? How could the Lord who is beyond space and time love creatures bounded by space and time such as us? It doesn't make sense. But that was just the beginning: God went on to declare his love for us in the cross of Jesus. In Jesus God not only entered human nature, but he experienced its most bitter element, death. And all this was for us. In the words of John again: 'he loved us and sent his Son to be the atoning sacrifice for our sins' (1 John 4:10). Here is love beyond measure, love that stands in such contrast to the tinsel of Christmas. For Santa Claus never died for anybody, but the babe of Bethlehem became the Christ of Calvary!

It may be that, in spite of all the merriment around this Christmas, we have come to church with little sense of joy: we may have laughed and smiled at others, but deep down within us there is perhaps an ache, if not a pain. In the last few days or weeks or months or maybe even years everything seems to have gone wrong; now our mind is in a whirl and we don't know what to think. 'Does anybody love me?' we ask. Yes, God does! The Word has become flesh. God has spoken a word of love; he wants to say to each one of us again as he did so many years ago: I love you, I sent my Son for you, I gave my Son for you. God, if we will but let him, wants, as it were, to put his arms around us and love us for all eternity. This is the Good News of Christmas.

God has come to us!

In Jesus God has come to us in grace. Three times in this brief passage John speaks of grace: the Word was 'full of grace' (1:14); 'from his fullness we have all received, grace upon grace' (1:16); 'The law . . . was given through Moses; grace . . . came through Jesus Christ' (1:17).

Grace has been defined as 'God's riches at Christ's expense'. Grace by definition is undeserved, it is unmerited, it is always free. Grace is never something we can earn, merit or attain; grace is always something that is given. In the coming of Jesus to our world we see God's love beyond deserving. There is no human reason why God should send his Son: it was love and love alone that caused Jesus to become one of us. What's more, he not only became one of us; he became one with us in our sin. He, the spotless Lamb of God, took upon himself the sin of the world: he died in our place that we might become one with God again. In the words of Irenaeus, an early church father: 'The Word of God, Jesus Christ, on account of His great love for mankind, became what we are in order to make us what He is Himself.'[22]

---

22. Irenaeus, *Against the Heresies* 3.19.1.

No wonder John speaks of our receiving 'grace upon grace'. God's grace in Jesus is boundless and inexhaustible. There is never a moment when God says, 'Enough is enough.' There is always sufficient grace to meet our need. So let us celebrate again the grace of God revealed in Jesus. In the words of the apostle Paul: 'You know the grace of our Lord Jesus Christ, that though he was rich, yet for your sakes he became poor, so that by his poverty you might become rich' (2 Cor. 8:9, marginal reading).

In Jesus God has also come to us in truth. Twice in this passage John describes Jesus in terms of truth: he was 'full of . . . truth' (1:14); not only grace, but also 'truth came through Jesus Christ' (1:17). 'Truth' is a term that appears a number of times in John. To his disciples Jesus says: 'I am . . . the truth' (14:6). Jesus also declares 'the truth will make you free' (8:32). To Pilate, Jesus says: 'I came into the world, to testify to the truth' (18:37), and Pilate goes on to ask, 'What is truth?' (18:38).

The truth Jesus came to reveal was the truth about God. But in revealing the truth about God, Jesus did not reveal some complex theological system; rather, he revealed himself. To all intents and purposes he said: 'See, this is what God is like.' Of course, the Christian faith is complicated. Nobody can ever fully understand God. We shall, in this world at least, never fully understand what it meant for Jesus to be fully man, and yet fully God. And yet, for all that, the truth of the gospel is surprisingly simple, for we only have to look at Jesus. The fact is that even the simplest mind can know God as intimately as the mind of the greatest philosopher. Today, in our mind's eye, let us look to Jesus again: see him in the manger at Bethlehem, see him by the lakeside in Galilee, see him on the cross of Calvary. Let us look, see and celebrate the truth of God's love in Jesus.

God has also come to us in glory: 'we have seen his glory, the glory as of a father's only son' (1:14). 'Glory' is another favourite word of John, which appears time and again in his Gospel. For example, at the end of recording the miracle of the water being turned into wine at the wedding of Cana, John comments: 'Jesus did this, the first of his signs, in Cana of Galilee, and revealed his glory' (John 2:11). Later, when Jesus learns that his friend Lazarus is ill, he says to his disciples: 'This illness . . . is for God's glory, so that the Son of God may be glorified through it' (John 11:3).

According to the English dictionary, the word 'glory' normally means either 'renown, fame' or 'beauty, majesty, magnificence, splendour'. But John means more than that. To understand what John was meaning, we have to remember that his thinking was steeped in the Old Testament. In the Old Testament, 'glory' refers to the visible presence of God. For example, after the tabernacle had been erected in the wilderness and its equipment installed we read: 'and the glory of the LORD filled the tabernacle' (Exod. 40:34). When Solomon's temple was dedicated, the priests could not enter it, 'for the glory of the LORD filled the house of the LORD' (1 Kgs 8:11). When Isaiah had his vision in the temple, he heard the angelic choir singing that 'the whole earth is full of his glory' (Isa. 6:3). Therefore, to see the glory of Jesus is to see God present in him.

This comes out also in John's phrase 'the Word lived among us' (1:14). The underlying Greek verb is associated with the Hebrew term for 'glory', šĕkînâ. The verb (eskēnōsen) is not the normal word for 'living'; rather, it is the word used for 'pitching a tent'. Indeed, we could translate it as 'the Word tabernacled among us'. That is, the glory that was present in the tabernacle of old was also present in Jesus. As God lived among people of old, first in the tabernacle and then in the wilderness, so in Jesus God came to live. In Jesus God was present.

Today we celebrate that 'we have seen his glory'. In the words of one commentator: 'The glory of God is not the glory of a despotic eastern tyrant, but that splendour of love before which we fall, not in abject terror, but lost in wonder, love and praise.'[23]

Finally, God has come to us in his Son: 'No one has ever seen God. It is God the only Son, who is close to the Father's heart, who has made him known' (1:18). When John said that nobody had ever seen God, everyone in the ancient world would have fully agreed with him. God was the great unknowable. In the Old Testament we read of God saying to Moses: 'you cannot see my face; for no one shall see me and live' (Exod. 33:20). But now, amazingly, God has made himself known in Jesus: in Jesus we see God.

Jesus is here described as God's 'only Son' (monogenēs). The AV

---

23. Barclay, The Gospel of John, I, p. 51.

speaks of God's 'only begotten Son'. Although this may be the literal meaning of the underlying Greek word, it had long lost its physical sense. Rather, it had come to have two special meanings. It had come to mean 'unique' and 'specially beloved'. The emphasis here is on the uniqueness of Jesus. So Peterson translates: 'This one-of-a-kind God-Expression' (*The Message*).

He has a special place in the Father's heart: 'God the only Son . . . is close to the Father's heart'. Literally, he is 'in the bosom of the Father'. 'To be in the bosom of someone' is the Hebrew phrase that expresses the deepest intimacy possible. It was used of a mother and child, of a husband and wife; it could also be used of very close friends. That is, Jesus is on intimate terms with God; indeed, he shares in the very life of God. It is this Jesus who has made God known. Interestingly, the underlying Greek verb *exegēsato* is related to the English term 'exegesis', which refers to the clarifying of the meaning in a text. John says that Jesus has expounded God. Jesus, if we like, has unpacked and clarified the love of God for all to see.

Yes, in Jesus, the distant, unknowable, invisible and unreachable God has come to us and made himself known. God can never be a stranger again! Hallelujah!

A meditation on grace and truth

Meditation has been defined as 'the activity of calling to mind and thinking over, and dwelling on, and applying to oneself, the various things one knows about the works and ways and purposes and promises of God'.[24] Or, to put it more simply, meditation involves using our minds to chew over all that God has done for us. It is so easy to hear what God has done for us, and not to hear it. Every year we come to church and hear the Christmas story read and sung to us, yet all too often we allow it to go in one ear and out the other. Today I want us to meditate on the Christmas story. I want us to do what Mary did after the visit of the shepherds, for Luke tells us that 'Mary treasured all these words and pondered them in her heart' (Luke 2:19). She 'turned them over in her mind' (J. B. Phillips) as she 'weighed up' what she had seen and heard. If you like, she 'meditated upon them'.

---

24. J. I. Packer, *Knowing God* (London: Hodder & Stoughton, 1973), p. 20.

As we call to mind the baby and the manger, the shepherds and the angels, the wise men and the star, let us listen to the way in which John summarizes the significance of this figure whose birth we celebrate: 'grace and truth came through Jesus Christ' (John 1:17). As we listen, let us think on it, dwell on it and apply it to ourselves.

First, 'grace came through Jesus Christ' (1:17). What is grace? Grace is love shown to the undeserving. The story is told of a small boy who had to apologize for forgetting his aunt's birthday. He wrote: 'I'm sorry I forgot your birthday. I have no excuse, and it would serve me right if you forgot mine, which is next Friday.' The aunt no doubt remembered his birthday: and in so doing exhibited grace, love totally undeserved. In Jesus God's grace takes human form. In the coming, living, dying and rising of Jesus, God shows his love for the undeserving, for people like us.

'Grace', said John Stott, 'is love that cares and stoops and rescues.' How true that is. In Jesus, God has shown us that he cares for us; in Jesus, God has stooped and became one of us; in Jesus, God has come to our rescue. For the good news is that the child in the manger became the Saviour on the cross. As the angel said to Joseph: 'You are to name him Jesus, for he will save his people from their sins' (Matt. 1:21).

'Grace came through Jesus Christ'. Let us take a moment and think on this, dwell on it and apply it to ourselves.

Secondly, 'truth came through Jesus Christ'. The American novelist Mark Twain wrote in his introduction to *The Adventures of Huckleberry Finn*: 'The Adventures of Tom Sawyer . . . was made by Mr Mark Twain, and he told the truth, mainly. There was things which he stretched, but mainly he told the truth.' But when Jesus spoke of God, he did not mainly speak the truth – he did not stretch things – everything that he spoke about God was true. Indeed, in a way that nobody else has ever dared to do, Jesus went on to claim to be the truth: 'I am the way, and the truth, and the life; no one comes to the Father except through me' (John 14:6). Jesus is the truth, in the sense that he – and he alone – reveals the full truth of God, and in so doing is the way, and so is the way to life. In Jesus our search for God is ended – for God has come to us in Jesus; and in Jesus the truth of God and his love is displayed.

Alas, all too often people shut their eyes to the truth, if they deem it inconvenient. Winston Churchill, for instance, once wrote of Stanley Baldwin: 'He occasionally stumbled over the truth, but hastily picked himself up and hurried on as if nothing had happened.'[25] Hopefully, this will not be so for us. My prayer is that none of us will rush off as if we had never encountered the truth. Rather, let us meditate upon the truth as it is in Jesus. Let us think on it, dwell on it, apply it to ourselves.

God's Christmas gift (John 3:16)

For God so loved the world that he gave his only Son, so that everyone who believes in him may not perish but may have eternal life.

Although we are looking at these words within the lens of Christmas, God's giving of his Son clearly embraces both his birth and his death: the entire mission of the Son is in view. Here we have a summary of the message of the Fourth Gospel, as indeed of the gospel itself.

'A little Bible'

Martin Luther once remarked that in the Bible there were a number of 'little Bibles': that is, verses or passages of Scripture which express in brief the good news to be found in its pages. John 3:16 is such a 'little Bible'. It contains the very heart of the gospel; it is a 'Gospel' within the Gospels.

Here we discover that the gospel begins with the love of God. We may think of the gospel as a great river of living water, flowing broad and deep for the life of all. If we trace that river back to its source, we discover that it springs from the love of God. As John wrote in his first letter: 'God's love was revealed among us in this way: God sent his only Son into the world so that we might live through him . . . He loved us and sent his Son to be the atoning sacrifice for our sins' (1 John 4:9–10). Or in the words of John 3:16: 'God so loved . . . that he gave'. It is this tremendous fact we celebrate. God declared his love,

---

25. J. L. Lane (ed.), *The Sayings of Winston Churchill* (London: Duckworth, 1992).

not merely in a spoken or written word, but in 'the Word made flesh'. In the words of Christina Rossetti's carol, 'Love came down at Christmas'.

Secondly, we discover that the gospel centres in the person of Christ. Right at the heart of our text we find Jesus, God's 'only Son'. Jesus is central to the gospel. Christianity is all about Christ! The Christian gospel is not primarily about a philosophical system or a moral code; it is about a person, the Jesus of history, who came into the world to save sinners.

Thirdly, we discover that the gospel ends with the gift of eternal life. The words of our text are so familiar that sometimes we fail to heed its sombre warning: apart from Jesus we are perishing. Apart from Jesus were are under a sentence of death, death that is the wages of our sin. But God in his infinite love has come to the rescue. He has given us his Son to die for us, so that our sins may be dealt with, and so that in turn we may enjoy a new living relationship with him. This is what 'eternal life' is actually all about. Eternal life is not simply life that goes on and on, but life of the age to come: that is, God's life; life lived in fellowship with God; life with the tang of eternity about it; life that can never die, because it is God's own life. Such a life is offered to those who believe and accept his Son. As John wrote in his first letter: 'God gave us eternal life, and this life is in his Son. Whoever has the Son has life; whoever does not have the Son of God does not have life' (1 John 5:11–12).

Beyond belief

Has anybody received the latest edition of the *Guinness Book of World Records* for Christmas?[26] It's a wonderful book full of all sorts of improbable but true facts. Such facts make for fascinating reading. But by and large they don't affect us. Yet there is one improbable, but nonetheless true, fact, unmentioned by the *Guinness Book of World Records*, that is of vital significance to every man, woman and child today: God loves us. Or as John puts it in his Gospel: 'For God so loved the world that he gave his only Son, so that everyone who believes in him may not perish but may have eternal life' (3:16).

---

26. *Guinness Book of World Records* (London: Guinness Superlatives, 50th ed., 2005).

The first improbable, but true, fact is that God loves the world, and not least us humans. That's a mind-boggling thought. The psalmist put it this way:

When I look at your heavens, the work of your fingers,
  the moon and the stars that you have established;
what are human beings that you are mindful of them,
  mortals that you care for them? (Ps. 8:3–4)

What indeed? We are so small and so insignificant. Just think of the size of the universe, galaxy upon galaxy – a universe so vast that measurement has no real meaning. Can you really imagine God taking an interest in our world, let alone in people like us? Furthermore, if God loves the world, then this means that he loves not just the best of us; he loves the worst of us too! Let's be honest: we are scarcely the most loveable of creatures, whatever our loved-ones might say. There is so much in us that is selfish and greedy, unloving and unkind. But God loves us. The wonder increases once we appreciate that the God who made the heavens and the earth is a holy God, whose 'eyes are too pure to behold evil' (Hab. 1:13) . It is this God, in whose presence sin can as much exist as ice in a fiery furnace, who loves us. It is almost beyond belief, and yet it is true.

How do we know it is true? This leads us on to a second equally improbable, but true, fact. God gave his only Son. At Christmas we remember the coming of Jesus to Bethlehem. But this was only the first stage of God showing his love for us all: for the babe of Bethlehem ended up as the Christ of Calvary. It was there on the cross that God showed his love most clearly for us. 'God so loved the world that he gave his only Son'. How could God love us so much? Some years ago my oldest son and his friends were asked this question in a 'philosophy' lesson at school: 'What would you do if you saw two people drowning in a river, one was your father, and the other a scientist on the verge of discovering the final cure for cancer – if you could save only one, which one would you save?' All the boys in my son's form said: 'My father'! The fact is that whatever anybody else may think about our children or our parents, we value members of our family far too highly to put somebody else before them. However awkward the children can get, however difficult our parents can get, there is nothing more precious than our family. But 'God gave his only Son' to die for us. God's love is almost beyond belief, and yet it is true. It is this that we celebrate on Christmas Day.

The third improbable, but true, fact is that God's gift is eternal life. For in this world nothing is eternal; nothing lasts. The carpet we were told would last a lifetime ultimately wears out; the car in which we invested a small fortune rusts away. We live today in a consumer society, where everything is built to fail. What is true of consumer 'durables' is also true of us. Centuries ago the psalmist wrote: 'The days of our life are seventy years, or perhaps eighty, if we are strong . . . they are soon gone, and we fly away' (Ps. 90:10). In spite of all the advances in modern medicine, this is still substantially true. Neither drugs nor surgery can prolong life indefinitely. Everything perishes. But Jesus offers eternal life. Needless to say, this is not mere prolongation of life. Who would want that? That would be hell itself. No, it's a new quality of life, life with God himself. If this isn't good news, then what is? What's more, this life can start this side of the grave. Life can begin again now. There can be a new dimension to life in the here and now. Christians may be in the world, but they are not of the world. If it all sounds highly improbable, then dare I suggest that this is only because we have never experienced it. As the playwright William Alfred once said: 'People who tell me there is no God are like a six year old saying there is no such thing as passionate love. They just haven't experienced him yet.'

The final improbable, but true, fact is that eternal life is for those who believe. For reason says: 'God would scarcely offer such a fantastic gift without conditions. Why, it would be like throwing pearls before swine. We surely must have to do something to deserve this gift of eternal life.' This is the attitude of religious people, both of followers of Islam and Judaism, as also of many nominal Christians here in Britain: if God is going to do something for us, then we have to work for it. 'God surely only gives eternal life to those who have lived a relatively good life, to those who have been good parents, to those who have done a good turn for a neighbour.' But no: our text declares that eternal life is for those who believe. If eternal life were for those who deserved it, then none of us would ever experience it; not even the most respectable of us would get a look in. For the Bible tells us very clearly that our best is not good enough. In the words of

Paul: 'all have sinned and fall short of the glory of God' (Rom. 3:23). The fact is that God's entry requirements for heaven are impossibly demanding. None of us can possibly get a grade A in everything we do. There is no way of getting into God's heaven through our own efforts. But thank God, we don't have to try to do the impossible. Jesus has done all that is necessary. He died on the cross that we might be forgiven. He has dealt with our sin. All we have to do is to believe. That may sound improbable, but it is true.

God today wants to give us a Christmas gift. But, like any other gift, it needs to be received. We need to accept God's offer of life. The story is told of a mentally retarded boy called John. John had few friends and no family, and he lived a tragically brief life. He died in agony after swallowing weedkiller by mistake. As he lay in hospital, he repeated over and over again John 3:16, a text he had learnt in Sunday school. But he repeated it in this way: 'For God so loved John that he gave his only Son that if John believes in him, John will not perish.' He made this verse his own. Will we do the same?

An overview: The real meaning of Christmas

Unlike Matthew, John does not tell of the wise men and star; and, unlike Luke, he does not tell of the angels and the shepherds. Indeed, he does not mention the virgin birth. But he does say that 'the Word became flesh and lived among us' (1:14), and in so doing he gets to the heart of the Christmas story.

Sadly, time and again people miss out on the heart of the Christmas story. For many, the word 'Christmas' conjures up parties and dances, pantomimes and nativity plays, Christmas trees with fairy lights, holly and mistletoe, Christmas stockings and presents, Christmas cards and letters, Santa Claus and reindeer, frost and snow, Christmas pudding and mince pies, Christmas dinner with turkey and Brussels sprouts. But these are but the trimmings. Strange as it may seem, in those parts of the world where these trimmings are not present, Christmas is celebrated with a good deal more fervour and enthusiasm than in the UK. For Christmas is not about mistletoe, Christmas trees and turkeys. As John points out, it is about the Word becoming flesh and living among us.

But if Christmas is not about the secular trimmings, nor is it about the religious 'trimmings'. The heart of the Christmas story is not about angels appearing to shepherds, nor about wise men following a star; it's not even about a baby born of a virgin. Do not get me wrong: I believe that angels did appear to shepherds; I believe that there was a star that guided wise men; I believe that Jesus was born of a virgin. But none of these events is essential to Christmas. Christmas would still be Christmas had there been no shepherds, had there been no wise men; nor, dare I say it, had there been no virgin birth. The wonder of Christmas is that God became man, 'the Word became flesh'. Here is the true wonder.

Sadly, the true meaning of Christmas can become lost even to Christian people. The distinguished German Lutheran bishop Hanns Lilje told of how in a Nazi prison in 1944 he celebrated Christmas with two fellow prisoners about to be executed: 'It is possible for the candles and lights to blind our eyes, so that we can no longer see the essential element in Christmas; but the people who "walk in darkness" can perhaps see it better than all who see only the lights of the earth.'[27] Stripped of all the 'trimmings', John's account of the incarnation gets to the heart of the Christmas story. And in so doing, he challenges us to respond in faith. For to all who receive the Christ, who believe in his name, he gives power to become children of God (1:12). Faith it has been said is the act of 'grasping reality': and the reality in question is Jesus, the Christ, the Son of God, the Word made flesh. It is only then with the eye of faith that we can pierce the fog of illusion and see the true wonder of the Christmas story.

---

27. Hanns Lilje, *The Valley of the Shadow* (ET London: SCM Press, 1950), pp. 84–85.

4 The Good News anticipated in the Old Testament

For Christians, the Old Testament does not stand on its own, but is a book about Jesus, in the sense that it prepares for the coming of the Messiah and the new people of God. And although Jesus may not be the principal subject of the Old Testament, nonetheless Christians have claimed that Jesus is the true fulfilment of all the hopes and expectations present in the Old Testament. In this regard it is significant that Jesus began his ministry by proclaiming: 'The time is fulfilled, and the kingdom of God has come near' (Mark 1:15). For Jesus the promise of the Old Testament was realized in his ministry. Not surprisingly, therefore, when after his resurrection Jesus meets with the two disciples on the Emmaus Road, 'beginning with Moses and all the prophets, he interpreted to them the things about himself in all the scriptures' (Luke 24:27). The good news of Jesus and the kingdom of God is indeed anticipated in the Old Testament.

However, as we shall see, although the good news of Jesus and the kingdom of God was anticipated, clarity of sight was inevitably lacking. Indeed, the words of Paul are applicable: 'now we see in a mirror, dimly' (1 Cor. 13:12). Time and again the prophets, for instance, when they spoke of the one to come, spoke more than they actually knew. But this is not surprising. For first and foremost the prophets had a message to bring to people of their own day. The prophets are not to be likened to a gypsy with her crystal ball, who seeks to predict the future. Their task was not to 'foretell' the future, but to 'forthtell' God's word. Any 'foretelling' was always secondary, taking place only within the context of 'forth-telling'.

The five Old Testament prophecies selected for exposition form the standard passages set down by most lectionaries to be read for the Christmas season. We shall seek to set these passages within their original context, then relate them to the coming of Christ, before showing how they might be of relevance to us today.

The sign of Immanuel (Isa. 7)

Thus says the Lord GOD . . .

> *If you do not stand firm in faith,*
> *you shall not stand at all. (Isa. 7:7a, 9b)*

'. . . *the Lord himself will give you a sign. Look, the young woman is with child and shall bear a son, and shall name him Immanuel. He shall eat curds and honey by the time he knows how to refuse the evil and choose the good. For before the child knows how to refuse the evil and choose the good, the land before whose two kings you are in dread will be deserted'. (Isa. 7:14–16)*

The context

The year was 735 BC. Assyria under Tiglath-pileser III was in the business of empire-building. A coalition had been formed against him, whose ringleaders were Rezin, king of Syria, and Pekah, king of Israel (7:1). Judah had been invited to become part of the coalition, but King Ahaz refused. Perhaps he felt that such a provocative action would not effectively stem Tiglath-pileser's advance, but would just put Judah into far greater danger. Then matters went from bad to worse. The allies decided to march against Jerusalem and remove Ahaz in favour of Tabeel, one of their own protégés (7:6). Ahaz and his people were scared stiff (7:2).

What should Ahaz do? As far as he could see, he hadn't a hope against the joint forces of Syria and Israel. Only one course of action seemed open to him: namely, to strip the treasury and send tribute to the Assyrian king, in the hope that by making himself Assyria's vassal Tiglath-pileser would come to his aid (2 Kgs 16:7–8). It was not the bravest of moves. It involved the selling out of the country's independence. But at least it would save Ahaz's position, if not his skin.

Isaiah, however, believed that there was another option open: Ahaz should turn to God and trust him. So, at the Lord's prompting, Isaiah set out to meet Ahaz 'at the end of the conduit of the upper pool' (7:3), where Ahaz was checking out the city's water-supply in preparation for the inevitable siege. Again, prompted by the Lord, Isaiah described the kings of Syria and Israel as 'two smouldering stumps of firebrands' (7:4), who would soon burn themselves out. How right Isaiah was: Syria was crushed in 732 BC. As for Israel, she lost her northern territories in 734 BC, her national existence in 722 BC, and ultimately lost her racial existence, so that by 670 BC Israel was 'no longer a people' (7:8).

Isaiah, therefore, told Ahaz not to panic or be afraid, for God was in control. Ahaz should just trust God: 'If you do not stand firm in faith, you shall not stand at all' (7:9). Believing was the way of surviving.

The sign of Immanuel

Ahaz was not convinced. So 'Again the LORD spoke to Ahaz, saying, Ask a sign of the LORD your God' (7:10–11). But Ahaz refused. Somewhat sanctimoniously he replied: 'I will not ask, and I will not put the LORD to the test' (7:12). Ahaz was in fact afraid to put the Lord to the test. His refusal to ask for a sign was a refusal to believe. He felt that the situation had got beyond God.

It is in this context that Isaiah said that if Ahaz would not ask for a sign, then God would take the initiative and give a sign: 'Look, the young woman is with child and shall bear a son, and shall name him Immanuel. He shall eat curds and honey by the time he knows how to refuse the evil and choose the good. For before the child knows how to refuse the evil and choose the good, the land before whose two kings you are in dread will be deserted' (7:14–16).

What was this sign? Traditionally, Christians have believed that Isaiah was prophesying the birth of Jesus (see Matt. 1:22–23). But if Isaiah was predicting the birth of Jesus, then how could it be a sign to

Ahaz? Ahaz would not see this sign in his own lifetime. From the perspective of Ahaz such a prophecy, if not a nonsense, would have been an irrelevance.

Much depends on how we translate and interpret Isaiah 7:14. 'Behold a virgin shall conceive' reads the Authorized Version. The NIV is very similar: 'The virgin will be with child'. But the Hebrew word itself ('almâ) simply denotes a young woman of marriageable age and says nothing about her lack of sexual activity. True, in the light of Israelite ethical and social standards, most girls covered by this term would have been virgins; but had the emphasis been on virginity, then Isaiah would surely have used the Hebrew word for virgin (bĕtûlâ).

Most modern versions use the definite article and suggest that Isaiah had a particular young woman in question: 'Look, the young woman will be with child'. The implication is that Isaiah was referring to someone whose identity was known both to him and to Ahaz, 'perhaps someone whom the king had recently married and brought into his harem';[1] alternatively, according to a Jewish tradition, Isaiah was referring to his own wife. There is something to be said for that latter suggestion, for this would mean that all his children had significant names: first Shearjashub (see Isa. 7:1–9); then Maher-shalal-hash-baz (Isa. 8:1–4) and Immanuel.

The NRSV favours a third option. Keeping the definite article, it translates the Hebrew in the present tense: 'Look, the young woman is with child' (NRSV). In so far as the verb 'to be' is absent in the Hebrew, this translation is possible. If so, then Isaiah was referring to something already in the process of happening.

One thing is for sure: Isaiah was not referring to an event seven hundred years away: he was looking to the immediate future. God was giving a sign now. What's more, before this child had reached the years of discretion and was able to distinguish good from evil, the enemies of Ahaz would be defeated. And by the time he was able to distinguish between good and evil, he would be eating 'curds and honey': that is, food rationing would be over, and there would be an abundance everywhere.

---

1. Raymond E. Brown, *The Birth of the Messiah: A Commentary on the Infancy Narratives in Matthew and Luke* (London: Geoffrey Chapman, 1977), p. 148.

The thrust of Isaiah's 'prophecy' was therefore this: 'Ahaz, put your trust in God, not in the might of Assyria. For in a short space of time prosperity and freedom will have returned again. As a sign of God's presence with you the young woman is (or shall be) with child and shall bear a son and shall name him Immanuel. Faith is the key.'

Isaiah was not referring to the future miracle of the incarnation, but to the fact that just as God had been with his people in the past, so he would continue to be with them. The birth of this child 'Immanuel' was an acted parable of his presence.

Jesus our Immanuel

So how does this tie in with the traditional association of Isaiah 7:14 with the birth of Jesus? Had Matthew got it wrong when in his account of the birth of Jesus he wrote: 'All this took place to fulfil what had been spoken by the Lord through the prophet:

> "Look, the virgin shall conceive and bear a son,
> and they shall name him Emmanuel"' (Matt. 1:22–23)?

No, Matthew had not got it wrong. Here we have a case of Isaiah speaking better than he knew; or rather, a case of a translator being inspired to produce a version that even more closely matched the birth of Jesus. For when the Hebrew text was translated into Greek some two hundred years before the birth of Jesus, the translator rendered the Hebrew word for young woman by the normal Greek word for 'virgin' (*parthenos*), a meaning the Hebrew could bear, but does not demand. Needless to say, it didn't take long for Christians like Matthew to spot the significance of this Greek word and to identify the 'prophecy' with the virginal conception of Jesus. Furthermore, along with this 'coincidence' of translation, there was also the incredibly appropriate title of Emmanuel, 'God with us'. What better description could there be of God incarnate!

But was this just an example of 'happy coincidence'? Can we honestly speak with Matthew of 'prophecy fulfilled'? Surely we can. For in fulfilling the prophecy beyond Isaiah's original intention, God did what he often does: he accomplished 'abundantly far more than all we can ask or imagine' (Eph. 3:20).

Isaiah looked forward to the day when God would intervene and save his people. In the coming of Jesus, God did indeed intervene; but far from saving his people from some external threat, he saved us from the deepest threat of all: namely, sin. In effect, what happened was the nature of God's salvation foretold by Isaiah was deepened, and the timing of God's salvation was lengthened. As the Swiss theologian Eduard Schweizer explained: 'Under certain kinds of illumination, a series of mountain ranges may be perceived as a single chain, without any suspicion of how many valleys lie between the first slope and the highest ridge; in like manner the prophets see God's saving work in the immediate and in the distant future as a single act.'[2]

Immanuel today

The question that the preacher faces is, how does this passage apply today? If the preacher is to respect the integrity of the original prophecy, then surely the emphasis must be on the necessity of faith: 'If you do not stand firm in faith, you shall not stand at all' (Isa. 7:9). This need to have faith in God can be applied in three ways in particular.

First, we are called to believe that God was in Christ; that in the birth of Jesus God was at work, seeking to bring about the salvation of the world. As Paul wrote to the Galatians: 'when the fullness of time had come, God sent his Son, born of a woman, born under the law, in order to redeem those who were under the law, so that we might receive adoption as children' (Gal. 4:4–5). But for that salvation to become effective in our lives, we need to believe, and to hang on to that belief!

Secondly, we are called to believe that God is with his church today. As truly as Ahaz felt threatened by the forces of Syria and Israel, so, too, many Christians feel threatened by the forces of secularism and irreligion. But God has not left us, and through his Spirit Jesus is present with us today (see Matt. 28:20). The key to the survival of the church is its faith in God. In this respect some words of the late Lord Clark at the end of his television lectures on civilization are pertinent: 'We can destroy ourselves by cynicism and disillusion, just as effectively as by

---

2. Eduard Schweizer, *The Good News according to Matthew* (ET London: SPCK, 1976), p. 32.

bombs.'[3] What is true of civilization is also true of the church. We need to believe, and hang on to that belief, that God is with us.

Thirdly, we are called to believe that God will be with us for ever. For the book of Revelation assures us, in the words of Isaiah 25:8, 35:10, that, when God restores all things at the end of time,

> God himself will be with them;
> he will wipe away every tear from their eyes.
> Death will be no more;
> mourning and crying and pain will be no more. (Rev. 21:3–4)

For those who believe, and hang on to that belief, there is a wonderful future.

So, as we hang up our decorations, write our cards and stir the pudding, let us say to ourselves: 'Immanuel – God was with us, God is with us, God will be with us.' Goodness, we'll want to keep up the decorations for ever!

A new king is coming! (Isa. 9:2–7)

> *The people who walked in darkness*
> *have seen a great light;*
> *those who lived in a land of deep darkness –*
> *on them light has shined.*
> *You have multiplied the nation,*
> *you have increased its joy;*
> *they rejoice before you*
> *as with joy at the harvest,*
> *as people exult when dividing plunder.*
> *For the yoke of their burden,*
> *and the bar across their shoulders,*
> *the rod of their oppressor,*
> *you have broken as on the day of Midian.*

---

3. Kenneth Clark, *Civilisation: A Personal View* (London: BBC and John Murray, 1969), p. 347.

For all the boots of the tramping warriors
    and all the garments rolled in blood
    shall be burned as fuel for the fire.
For a child has been born for us,
    a son given to us;
authority rests upon his shoulders;
    and he is named
Wonderful Counsellor, Mighty God,
    Everlasting Father, Prince of Peace.
His authority shall grow continually,
    and there shall be endless peace
for the throne of David and his kingdom.
    He will establish and uphold it
with justice and with righteousness
    from this time onward and for evermore.
The zeal of the LORD of hosts will do this.

Light has come to our darkness

When Isaiah first spoke these words, there was much darkness. The Assyrian king, Tiglath-pileser III, in the years 734–732 BC, had conquered the northern provinces of Israel, 'Zebulun and the land of Naphtali' (9:1) and had turned them into Assyrian provinces.

In effect, Isaiah's prophecies of gloom and doom had been fulfilled. For he had declared that God would judge his people Israel because they had turned their back upon him and upon his ways (see, for instance, Isa. 1:24–25). And this is precisely what happened. God used Assyria to crush Israel; judgment was not left to the end of time: it became a reality within history. There was indeed much darkness.

But Isaiah was also a prophet of hope. Light will come to our darkness. Indeed, he was so certain of the coming of light that he used what is known as a 'prophetic past tense' and spoke of it as a present event. 'The people who walked in darkness have seen a great light' (Isa. 9:2). At the time Isaiah was speaking the light had not actually come. But as he looked towards the coming of the light, the future was so real and vivid in his mind that, as far as he was concerned, the future had already arrived: God had already accomplished his purpose.

Was Isaiah able to look some seven hundred or more years ahead? Did he in his mind's eye see the light Jesus would bring? No, first and foremost Isaiah was speaking to his contemporaries. If Isaiah had been told that his prophecy would be fulfilled only after a gap of almost eight centuries, he would have been most surprised. But this is not to deny the validity of the prophecy. Rather, it is a cause of reverent wonder that God should so miraculously fulfil the prophecy in the way he did.

Isaiah described the coming of the Messiah in terms of light bursting forth on the darkness of Galilee (Isa. 9:1). Matthew in his Gospel (Matt. 4:15–16) used these words of the ministry of Jesus in Galilee. It was particularly appropriate that those provinces of Israel that were the first to fall to the Assyrian Empire should have been the first to receive the good news of the kingdom from the lips of the Messiah himself. But the light that came to the darkness of northern Israel was not restricted to Israel. For Jesus came to bring light to the world. John in his Gospel rightly applied the metaphor of light to the world in general: 'in him was life and the life was the light of all people. The light shines in the darkness, and the darkness did not overcome it' (John 1:4–5).

At this point the preacher can apply this 'prophecy' to the way in which Jesus brings light to our world too. For we live in a dark world marked by much pain and suffering: a world that is characterized by disappointment and frustration, despair and hopelessness. Into a world as dark as death, Jesus the light of the world has come. In him there is hope. In him there is life. Here is good news.

Joy has dispelled sorrow

The opening words of Isaiah 9:3 vary from one version to another. Some versions speak of the nation being multiplied (so NRSV); others of joy being multiplied (so GNB). It may be that there is little difference between the two ways of reading the verse. A nation that had been depopulated through war would indeed rejoice if there were an increase in the birthrate. Whatever the precise meaning of the opening phrase, the thrust of the whole verse is clear: joy has dispelled sorrow.

Isaiah uses two particular images to depict the greatness of the joy. The first image is the joy of harvest: 'they rejoice . . . as with joy at the harvest' (Isa. 9:3b). For us this imagery is not all that telling: our food supply is such that we have become more or less independent of the seasons. But in Isaiah's time, as still for many people in the world today, harvest signified the end of a long period of hunger. 'The days spent on the threshing floor are the most joyful in the whole year for the farmer and his family, and indeed for the whole village.'[4] The second image is the joy of dividing up the booty after a successful military expedition: 'they rejoice . . . as people exult when dividing plunder' (Isa. 9:3c). Again we are dealing with an image from the past; perhaps the nearest some of us have ever got to this is when we went scrumping as children and after a successful raid divided up the proceeds!

With the coming of the promised Messiah, declared Isaiah, the sorrow associated with the past will be done away with: instead, there will be 'great joy' (Isa. 9:3, GNB). And such proved to be the case. As the angel said to the shepherds: 'see – I am bringing you good news of great joy for all the people: to you is born this day in the city of David a Saviour, who is the Messiah, the Lord' (Luke 2:10–11).

What was true then is true today. For Jesus today can turn our sorrow into joy. Jesus still can save us from the vicious spiral of sin and death. Whatever the mess we have made of our past, Jesus can deal with it. With him, our present and our future are secure.

Defeat has been turned to victory

Isaiah pictured Israel bowed down with the financial burden of having to pay tribute to the Assyrians; of being forced to work for the Assyrians as an animal might be driven by a stick. But suddenly the picture changes. This burdensome yoke of foreign rule will be shattered. Israel will be set free, victory will come 'as on the day of Midian' (Isa. 9:4).

The 'day of Midian' refers to the time when Gideon with only 300 men defeated the Midianites camped in the plain of Jezreel (see Judg. 7). What happened then will happen again, declared Isaiah; God will free his people again. When the Messiah comes, he will break the yoke of foreign domination. What is more, the victory, far from being short-lived, will be final. It will be permanent. For when Gideon defeated the Midianites, it was only a temporary victory. It wasn't

---

4. H. Guthe, quoted by Otto Kaiser, *Isaiah 1–12* (ET London: SCM Press, 1972), p. 127.

long before Israel was in trouble again. But the day will come when warriors will throw away their boots and their bloodstained military cloaks; instead of storing them up to await the next battle, they will be burned (Isa. 9:5). When the Messiah comes, his victory will be permanent. He will inaugurate a kingdom that will have no end.

In a way that Isaiah could never have dreamt, we can apply these words to Jesus. For Jesus, the Messiah, came to do battle not with human forces, but with spiritual forces. Every Sunday we celebrate that in his cross and resurrection Jesus defeated the powers of sin and death; and not just for the time being, but for ever.

For to us a child is born

Isaiah's hopes of light, joy and victory are placed in the coming of the Messiah, who will establish and uphold 'the throne of David and his Kingdom' (Isa. 9:7). This coming Messiah is described in a series of four epithets.[5]

The coming king, declared Isaiah, can be described as a 'Wonderful Counsellor'. The precise sense of the adjective is uncertain: the Hebrew could be translated as 'wonderful' or 'supernatural'. Whatever the correct meaning, this new ruler will not need others to advise him as to how he administers his royal power. When it comes to wisdom, he will be self-sufficient. How true this proved to be in the coming of Jesus. The crowds marvelled as he taught them with authority: an authority that came not from formal rabbinic training, but from within himself.

The Messiah can also be described as 'Mighty God' or 'Mighty Hero' (REB), in the sense that he proves to be superior to all on the battlefield. He mops up the enemy with ease. Jesus the Messiah, through his cross and resurrection, was able to do battle on our behalf against the powers of evil and to triumph (see Col. 2:15), precisely because he was the Son of God.

He is the 'Everlasting Father'. At first sight this appears an unusual epithet if we are to apply it to Jesus, the Son of God. However, there is no need to press the metaphor. There is no confusion between the

---

5. The AV treats the term 'Wonderful' as a separate name from 'Counsellor': actually the two belong together.

Father and the Son. The Son is the Everlasting Father in the sense that he cares for his people as a father cares for his children. Indeed, 'Father of the people' was a term often applied to a great leader of a Middle Eastern nation, in the sense that he was a beneficent as distinct from a despotic ruler.

Finally, the Messiah is the 'Prince of Peace'. Isaiah goes on to describe how 'His authority shall grow continually, and there shall be endless peace' (Isa. 9:7). Jesus too came as the Prince of Peace (see Zech. 9:9–10); as the great Colossian Christ-hymn declares, he made 'peace through the blood of his cross' (Col. 1:20: see Eph. 2:14)

This is no pipe-dream, declared Isaiah: 'The zeal of the LORD of hosts will do this' (Isa. 9:7). And in God's good time, God well and truly fulfilled this promise.

The dream of God's kingdom (Isa. 11:1–9)

A shoot shall come out from the stock of Jesse,
and a branch shall grow out of his roots.
The spirit of the LORD shall rest on him,
the spirit of wisdom and understanding,
the spirit of counsel and might,
the spirit of knowledge and the fear of the LORD.
His delight shall be in the fear of the LORD.

He shall not judge by what his eyes see,
or decide by what his ears hear;
but with righteousness he shall judge the poor,
and decide with equity for the meek of the earth;
he shall strike the earth with the rod of his mouth,
and with the breath of his lips he shall kill the wicked.
Righteousness shall be the belt around his waist,
and faithfulness the belt around his loins.

The wolf shall live with the lamb,
the leopard shall lie down with the kid,
the calf and the lion and the fatling together,
and a little child shall lead them.

The cow and the bear shall graze,
   their young shall lie down together;
   and the lion shall eat straw like the ox.
The nursing child shall play over the hole of the asp,
   and the weaned child shall puts its hand on the adder's den.
They will not hurt or destroy
   on all my holy mountain;
for the earth will be full of the knowledge of the LORD
   as the waters cover the sea.

Isaiah had a dream

In the eighth century BC Isaiah had a dream of a new David, a Messiah-king who would restore Israel's fortunes (11:1). At the time when Isaiah was dreaming, Israel was on its beam-ends. Her very existence as a nation was under threat. God was using the emperor of Assyria to punish Israel for its sins (see 10:6). The northern kingdom of Israel had already been taken over by Assyria. The southern kingdom of Judah was threatened. It was a depressing and frightening time to be alive. Into this situation Isaiah spoke a word of hope. The time is coming, said Isaiah, when the Lord will punish Assyria too. 'The LORD Almighty will bring them [the Assyrians] crashing down like branches cut off a tree. The proudest and highest of them will be cut down and humiliated' (10:33, GNB). It is within that context that Isaiah then spoke of a 'shoot' coming out from the stump of Jesse (Isa. 11:1). Assyria will be cut down, never to rise again. But Israel is felled, only to have new life emerge from its stump. For, from this stump, a new king will arise.

This new king will possess an ideal character and will be unusually gifted (11:2).

> In the power of the spirit, the future king will have no need of human advisers, with their selfish attempts to influence him. His judicial wisdom and ability to distinguish between appearances and reality will enable him to plan aright, and he will also possess the power to translate his decisions into action: for upon him rests the spirit of counsel and heroic might.[6]

---

6. Kaiser, *Isaiah 1–12*, p. 158.

What's more, says Isaiah: 'his delight shall be in the fear of the LORD' (11:3). The king will not be proud and arrogant; rather, he will be devout and righteous, knowing that he must ultimately give an account of his actions to God himself. Not surprisingly, therefore, this king will protect the interest of the poor and vulnerable members of society (Isa. 11:3b–4). Isaiah had a vision of a truly fair society.

But Isaiah went even further in his dreaming. He dreamt not just of an ideal nation, but of an ideal world: a world in which everybody would be at peace with one another (Isa. 11:6–9). At first sight this passage is about the natural order changing radically: of wolves being at peace with lambs, of lions being at peace with oxen, of the animal kingdom no longer being a threat to humankind, of Eden being restored. However, it may be that Isaiah was using this vivid series of metaphors to speak not so much about relationships in the animal kingdom, but rather about relationships between men and women. Elsewhere in the Old Testament, for instance, wolves represent fierceness and oppression (e.g. Gen. 49:27; Zeph. 3:3), while 'a lamb led to the slaughter' stands for helplessness (e.g. Jer. 11:19). John Sawyer therefore writes:

> It seems therefore more likely that this prophecy is not literally about the taming of wild animals and the removal of natural dangers from the countryside, but about a new age in which old enmities will be forgotten, the mighty will live peacefully with the weak (v6), ruthless exploiters of the poor and needy will change their habits (v7), and the vulnerable will be immune from danger (v8). Verse 9 sums it all up in the two words translated 'hurt' and 'destroy': there will be no more ill-treatment or corruption in Zion . . . It is the vision of a new world characterized by justice, righteousness and peace.[7]

If so, then Isaiah dreamt of a second David, an ideal king, who would inaugurate a universal age of peace. On that day God would be known, and his rule would be experienced, everywhere: 'the earth

---

7. John F. A. Sawyer, *Isaiah*, I, Daily Study Bible (Edinburgh: St Andrew Press, 1984), p. 123.

will be full of the knowledge of the LORD as the waters cover the sea'
(11:9b). What a dream!

Giving shape to the dream

At Christmas we celebrate the coming of Jesus, the Messiah the Son
of David, and as we do so we celebrate that Isaiah's dream has begun
to take shape. But that dream has yet to materialize fully. The
kingdom of God may have come, but it has yet to be established for
all to see. The day has still to arrive when the age-old battles between
good and evil are over; when not only will nation never again go to
war against nation, but also when people everywhere will be at peace
with one another.

But the dream is not just a future hope, for already in the here and
now God's kingdom is beginning to take shape. First and foremost,
this hope is being realized in God's church. For in Christ 'there is no
longer Jew or Greek, there is no longer slave or free, there is no
longer male and female'. All the old enmities and rivalries are done
away with. 'All of you are one in Christ Jesus' (Gal. 3:28) wrote Paul.
That is the reality. But it is a reality that God's people constantly need
to work at. In the words of one of the key ecumenical texts of the
late twentieth century, adopted by churches of every tradition:

> The eucharistic celebration demands reconciliation and sharing among all
> those regarded as brothers and sisters in the one family of God and is a con-
> stant challenge in the search for appropriate relationships in social, economic
> and political terms . . . As participants in the eucharist, therefore, we prove
> inconsistent if we are not actively participating in this ongoing restoration of
> the world's situation and the human condition.[8]

Giving shape to this dream is not easy. It is, for instance, not always
easy to love one another. The German philosopher Schopenhauer
likened people to a pack of porcupines on a freezing winter night.
The subzero temperature forces them together for warmth. But as
soon as they press very close, they jab and hurt one another. So they

---

8. *Baptism, Eucharist and Ministry*, Faith & Order Paper No. 111 [The Lima
Document] (Geneva: World Council of Churches, 1982), p. 14.

separate, only to attempt, in vain, over and over again, to huddle together. Loving can be painful. For Jesus it meant a crown of thorns and the agony of the nails. Sometimes we are tempted to withdraw from one another rather than to put up with the discomfort, if not the pain, of being brothers and sisters to one another; but to withdraw from one another is to give up on loving; it is to give up on the dream.

Jesus wants us to give shape to the dream. For in giving shape to the dream we offer a sign – if not proof – to the world that there is a new world coming, a world where Jesus is king, where peace and harmony reign.

The ruler from Bethlehem (Mic. 5:2–5)

> *But you, O Bethlehem of Ephrathah,*
> *who are one of the little clans of Judah,*
> *from you shall come forth for me*
> *one who is to rule in Israel,*
> *whose origin is from of old,*
> *from ancient days.*
> *Therefore he shall give them up until the time*
> *when she who is in labour has brought forth;*
> *then the rest of his kindred shall return*
> *to the people of Israel.*
> *And he shall stand and feed his flock in the strength of the* LORD,
> *in the majesty of the name of the* LORD *his God.*
> *And they shall live secure, for now he shall be great*
> *to the ends of the earth;*
> *and he shall be the one of peace.*

Bethlehem is a small Judean village, some five or six miles to the south of Jerusalem. It stands on a grey limestone ridge, more than 2,500 feet up. Surrounded by fertile countryside, it lived up to its name, 'house of bread'.

This village of Bethlehem was also known as 'Ephrath' or 'Ephrathah' after the clan of Ephrath or Ephrathah, an ally of Caleb (1 Chr. 2:19, 24, 50), which settled in the area. The family of Elimelech and Naomi are described as 'Ephrathites from Bethlehem' (Ruth 1:2);

and David is similarly described as 'the son of an Ephrathite of Bethlehem in Judah' (1 Sam. 17:12). This double identification was necessary to distinguish Bethlehem in Judah from Bethlehem in Zebulun (Josh. 19:15).

Although today Bethlehem is now known all over the world, it was an insignificant place: but 'one of the little clans of Judah'. Its insignificance is seen in the fact that it was not even mentioned in a list of place-names in Judah when Joshua divided the land (Josh. 15:20–63). It was put on the map, however, by David: for David hailed from Bethlehem (1 Sam. 16:1–13); and when David was on the run from Saul, it was 'water . . . from the well of Bethlehem' that David longed to drink (2 Sam. 23:15).

Precisely because of David's associations with Bethlehem, it is not surprising that Micah declared that the messianic ruler who would fulfil the promises given to David (see 2 Sam. 7) would come from Bethlehem. Micah is probably alluding to this link with David when he describes the origin of this 'one who is to rule in Israel' as 'from old, from ancient days' (5:2) – or as the GNB renders it, 'whose family line goes back to ancient times'. The suggestion that Micah is also alluding to a supernatural origin for this ruler is unlikely, even although the same terminology is used of God in Habakkuk 1:12.

The coming of this ruler will, however, be delayed until after God's people have paid the price for their wicked ways (see Mic. 2:1–11). Micah is a prophet of judgment: God will 'give up' his people to the consequences of their sin (see Rom. 1:24, 26, 28). But Micah is also a prophet of hope. He likens Israel's sufferings to the pain of childbirth, which ultimately gives way to the joy of new birth: 'then the rest of his kindred shall return' from exile (5:3), and the fortunes of Israel will be restored.

On that day justice and security will return to Israel. Whereas the old shepherds had 'fleeced' the flock (see Mic. 3:1–3), this ruler will 'feed his flock'. The picture of a ruler as a shepherd was a common one (see, for instance, Ezek. 34). Sometimes the shepherd can also be a figure for the Lord (Isa. 40:11; Ps. 23). Here, however, the ruler is God's representative who will rule 'in the majesty of the name of the LORD his God' Mic. 5:4). The hopes of peace, already expressed in Micah 4:1–4 will now be fulfilled, for 'he shall be the one of peace' (Mic. 5:5a).

For the preacher a number of themes suggest themselves. First,

God chooses the weak and insignificant. The powerful and sophisticated might have thought God would have chosen Jerusalem: but God turns his back on the 'metropolis' and instead chooses insignificant Bethlehem. What was true then was true when Jesus was born. From the perspective of the powerful and sophisticated of that day, Bethlehem (as indeed Judea) was a backwater: but it was in Bethlehem of Judea that Jesus was born. At Corinth God again 'chose what is weak in the world to shame the strong' (1 Cor. 1:27). And today God continues to choose to use the weak and insignificant. The fact that we do not perceive ourselves to be important does not mean to say that God has not got important things to do through us.

Secondly, God keeps his promises. In a way that was beyond Micah's wildest imaginings, God's Messiah did come from Bethlehem. The degree to which God fulfilled some of the details of this prophecy is debated. Some, for instance, have seen an allusion to the birth of Jesus in the birth-pangs of Judah; and a reference to the effects of Augustus' census in the flow of peoples back to Israel. The thrust of the passage, however, is clear: a ruler will come from Bethlehem. Here we have an illustration of Paul's words that in Jesus 'every one of God's promises is a "Yes"' (2 Cor. 1:20). 'God is faithful' (1 Cor. 1:9): we can depend on him.

Thirdly, however tough life may be at present, God has a wonderful future in store. 'He shall be the one of peace' (Mic. 5:5a). The day will come when nations 'shall beat their swords into plough shares, and their spears into pruning hooks' (Mic. 4:3) and war shall be no more. The day too shall come when all will 'sit under their own vines and under their own fig trees' (Mic. 4:4) and economic oppression shall be no more. The kingdom of God will be characterized by the security, prosperity and well-being which belong to the 'peace' that God's Messiah will bring.

An overview: Dreaming of peace

Martin Luther King had a dream, a dream that

> one day on the red hills of Georgia the sons of former slaves and the sons of former slave-owners will be able to sit down together at the table of brother-

hood . . . I have a dream that my four little children will one day live in a nation where they will not be judged according to the colour of their skin but by the content of their character . . . I have a dream that one day every valley shall be exalted, and every hill and mountain shall be made low, the rough places shall be made plain, and the crooked places will be made straight, and the glory of the Lord shall be revealed and all flesh shall see it.[9]

Isaiah and Micah likewise had a dream; they dreamt of a day when war would be no more, and peace would be the order of the day. In all four passages under review this dream is present.

Like Isaiah and Micah, we too dream of a day when war will be no more. In a world that has become a global village we dream of peace for our neighbours. We dream, for instance, of peace in Israel, peace in Iraq and peace in Afghanistan; we dream too of peace in the Sudan and peace in Zimbabwe. War is such a dreadful business. For war brings only pain, misery and waste:

> Waste of Muscle, waste of Brain,
> Waste of Patience, waste of Pain,
> Waste of Manhood, waste of Health,
> Waste of Beauty, waste of Wealth,
> Waste of Blood, and waste of Tears,
> Waste of Youth's most precious years,
> Waste of ways the Saints have trod,
> Waste of Glory, waste of God – War![10]

These lines penned by G. A. Studdert-Kennedy, popularly known as 'Woodbine Willie', who served as a chaplain to the forces in the First World War, are as true today as ever.

Of course, war is not the only evil. There are hunger and disease, poverty and ignorance. But how much more could be done to alleviate these but for the crippling cost of war, past, present and to come: every year thousands of millions of pounds are spent on armaments.

---

9. Speech made in Washington, 28 August 1963.
10. G. A. Studdert-Kennedy, 'Waste', in *More Rough Rhymes of a Padre* (London: Hodder & Stoughton, 1919).

The former soldier and US President Dwight Eisenhower once said: 'Every gun that is fired, every warship launched, every rocket fired, signifies, in the final sense, a theft from those who hunger and are not fed, those who are cold and are not clothed.' He went on: 'The world in arms is not spending money alone. It is spending the sweat of its labourers, the genius of its scientists, the hopes of its children.'[11]

But the four passages we have studied have a lesson for us. Our dreams of peace must not be disassociated from the coming of the kingdom of God and of his Messiah. In all four passages the promise of peace and of well-being is inextricably linked with the reign of God and of his Messiah. Only then will there be a cessation of political and economic oppression; only then will there be an end to hateful and divisive ideology; only then will they learn – and practise – peace. On the cornerstone of a wall at the United Nations headquarters in New York these words of Isaiah 2:4 and Micah 4:3 are inscribed: 'They shall beat their swords into ploughshares. And their spears into pruning hooks. Nation shall not lift up sword against nation. Neither shall they learn war any more.' But as Isaiah and Micah make clear, this peace will become a reality only when the nations are willing to submit to God's teaching that comes 'out of Zion' (Isa. 2:3; Mic. 4:2) where the one true God has revealed himself. This is not to denigrate the United Nations and its work. The United Nations does reduce conflict between nations; our world would be much worse without the United Nations. But a united world – a true league of nations – will happen only when God's kingdom comes, when God's Messiah returns to transform God's world. Then, when the 'Prince of Peace' is on the throne, 'there shall be endless peace' (Isa. 9:6, 7); then everyone 'shall live secure' (Mic. 5:4).

This hope of world peace has yet to materialize; the kingdom of God has yet to arrive in all its fullness. And yet there is a difference between us and the prophets. For the good news of Christmas is that with the coming of Jesus a beach-head of the kingdom has been established in our world. So the angels sang of the 'peace' that God now offers us all (Luke 2:14). So Paul could write to the Ephesians:

---

11. Speech in Washington, 16 April 1953, in *Public Papers of Presidents 1953* (1960), p. 182.

'he [i.e. Christ – the Messiah!] is our peace', for by his death on the cross Jesus has 'broken down the dividing wall, that is, the hostility between us' (Eph. 2:14). The hostility Paul had in mind was the division between Jew and Gentile, a division that was as sharp then as the division between Israeli and Palestinian is today. But just as in the first century even the bitterest of divisions were overcome in Christ, so too today in the twenty-first century the bitterest of divisions may, and indeed can be, overcome in Christ. As the people of God we are called to be a pointer to the coming kingdom of God.

There is a place for dreaming of peace. But the dream of peace must not be disassociated from the coming of the kingdom. For without God, the dream remains but a dream. But with God, the dream can – and will – become a reality.

5 The Good News reflected upon in the Epistles

In so far as the Epistles in general are a reflection upon the difference that the coming of Jesus has made to our world, it is almost an impossible task to make an appropriate selection of passages from them. Inevitably, therefore, the following selection is somewhat subjective.

The very act of selecting passages from the Epistles, however, is a reminder that preaching at Christmas need not be restricted to the Gospels. Indeed, we are the poorer if we limit our preaching simply to the Gospels, for in many ways the Epistles offer greater theological depth. Crudely put, the Gospels tell the story; the Epistles reflect upon it.

Freedom begins in Bethlehem (Rom. 8:3)

For God has done what the law, weakened by the flesh could not do: by sending his own Son in the likeness of sinful flesh, and to deal with sin, he condemned sin in the flesh.

Imagine turning up at court, with your suitcase all packed, knowing that the jury would have no other option but to find you guilty and that the judge consequently would have no other option but to send you down for life, and then all of a sudden having the verdict and sentence quashed. You would be over the moon! You would hug your barrister, kiss your solicitor and then bounce off to the nearest hotel to celebrate. Instead of going to gaol and serving time, you would be free, free to live. In essence, this is what Paul has in mind here in Romans 8: 'There is therefore now no condemnation for those who are in Christ Jesus' (8:1). The good news for those who have put their trust in the Lord Jesus is that they are no longer under God's judgment. They are free, free to live.

The fact is that all of us, religious and non-religious people alike, stand guilty before God: 'All have sinned and fall short of the glory of God' (Rom. 3:23). Unlike those school reports that used to say 'room for some improvement', this report on our standing before God says 'there is no hope at all'. The Swiss theologian Emil Brunner put it this way:

> A 'sinner' does not signify that there is something bad in him, as a splendid apple may have a little bad speck that can be removed with a twist of the paring knife . . . rather, we have been infected with evil at the core. 'All are sinners' does not mean that even the best are not quite saints. It means rather that the difference between the so-called good and the so-called bad no longer comes into consideration.[1]

But the good news is that 'There is . . . now no condemnation for those who are in Christ Jesus'. How has this come about? God, declares Paul, has sent 'his own Son in the likeness of sinful flesh, and to deal with sin' (Rom. 8:3). Freedom begins with Bethlehem.

Here then we have an incarnational statement that corresponds to John 1:14: 'the Word became flesh'. Yet there is a difference: for Paul doesn't simply state that Jesus took upon himself our human nature; he uses the somewhat strange expression 'in the likeness of sinful flesh'. Some have deduced that these words indicate that Paul didn't believe that Jesus became truly man, and think they indicate that Paul

---

1. Emil Brunner, *Our Faith* (ET London: SCM Press, 2nd ed., 1949), p. 41.

was a 'docetist': that is, Paul was saying that Jesus appeared to be a man, but in actual fact was not. That argument is difficult to swallow, for elsewhere in this letter Paul makes it abundantly clear that Jesus did take upon himself our flesh and blood. For example, he draws upon an early confession of faith to describe Jesus as 'descended from David according to the flesh' (1:3); later he speaks without reservation of the man Christ Jesus (see 5:17).

Jesus involved himself fully in our human situation. Jesus shared our flesh and blood. He knew, for instance, what it was like to feel pain: the nailing of his body to the cross was as much agony to him as it was to the two thieves crucified either side of him. He knew what it was like to experience temptation, perhaps not least the temptation to 'choose the easier path and to win the allegiance of his contemporaries by showing them signs, [this] was a real temptation to do wrong, and it came to Christ as a result of the sin of others, being due to their hardness of heart'.[2]

Jesus assumed our human nature. And yet, as Paul hints, our human nature was never the whole story: for Jesus never ceased to be the eternal Son of God. Hence, although he was tempted, he was able to resist temptation. Jesus came 'in the likeness of sinful flesh'. The presence of the adjective 'sinful' is significant. Jesus assumed our flesh, but without sin. He shared our human nature, but not our sinful human nature. In the words of 2 Corinthians 5:21 he 'knew no sin'. The fact is that unless Jesus had been sinless, he could not have been our Saviour; had he shared our sinful human nature, then he would himself have been in need of being saved. But we are not set free by his sinless life alone; his sinless life is a precondition for the cross to have saving power.

So from the incarnation, Paul turns to the cross. God sent 'his own Son . . . to deal with sin', and in so doing 'he condemned sin in the flesh'. Leon Morris comments: 'We should take "in the flesh" with "condemned" rather than with "sin"; we are not to think that "sin in the flesh" is condemned and other sin is not. It was what Jesus did "in the flesh" that condemned all sin.'[3]

---

2. D. E. H. Whiteley, *The Theology of St Paul* (Oxford: Blackwell, 1964), p. 135.

3. Leon Morris, *The Epistle to the Romans* (Leicester: IVP, 1988), p. 303.

Paul is now picturing sin as a litigant in a law-court; the verdict goes against sin and thus sin is condemned. Condemned here means more than that a form of words goes against our sin: there is also the thought that condemnation is brought into effect (just as when a derelict building is 'condemned', it is used no more and demolition follows). But it may be that an additional picture is present, and that the law-court scene is combined with a scene from the temple. Other versions speak of God sending his own Son 'to be a sin offering' (NIV) or 'a sacrifice for sin' (NEB). The underlying Greek phrase (*peri hamartias*) by itself does not justify a reference to the Jewish sacrificial system. But in the Septuagint, the Greek version of the Old Testament, this phrase regularly translates the Hebrew expression for 'sin-offering'; for example, Isaiah 53:10 'he makes his Life an offering for sin'. Paul, steeped as he was in the Old Testament Scriptures, probably saw the death of Jesus in sacrificial terms. God dealt with sin by sending his own Son to be a sin-offering. There on the cross Jesus dealt with sin by taking our place and in his body experiencing God's holy judgment against sin.

So then, we are set free by the coming and dying of Jesus. Or, to be precise, 'for those who are in Christ Jesus' there is 'now no condemnation'. It is those who have entrusted their lives to Jesus who may experience freedom from sin and death. It is those who have their faith in Jesus, who may hold their heads high on the Day of Judgment.

The Christmas jackpot (2 Cor. 8:9)

For you know the generous act [grace] of our Lord Jesus Christ, that though he was rich, yet for our sakes he became poor, so that by his poverty you might become rich.

Jules Feiffer, an American humorist, once wrote:

> I used to think I was poor. Then they told me I wasn't poor, I was needy. Then they told me it was self-defeating to think of myself as needy, I was deprived. Then they told me deprived was a bad image, I was underprivileged. Then they told me underprivileged was overused, I

was disadvantaged. I still don't have a dime. But I sure have a great vocabulary![4]

Whatever word we use, there are few who would argue the advantages of having nothing to your name. In the words of the eighteenth-century English clergyman Sydney Smith: 'Poverty is no disgrace to a man, but it is confoundedly inconvenient.'[5]

The result is that we all long for more, particularly at Christmas, when there seem to be so many people for whom we have to buy presents. What a difference it would make if we were to hit the jackpot, if our number were to come up in the Lottery draw. Just think of the difference £10 million would make to life. But would £10 million really make us that happy? Aristotle Onassis, the Greek shipping tycoon, said just before he died: 'I've just been a machine for making money. I seem, to have spent my life in a golden tunnel looking for the outlet which would lead to happiness. But the tunnel kept going on. After my death there will be nothing left.' Much of his money was left to his daughter, Christine Onassis. But she doesn't seem to have been any happier. On more than one occasion she seriously attempted suicide. True riches, and therefore presumably true happiness, says Paul, is found in Jesus, who embraced poverty in order that we might become rich; not rich in terms of hard cash, but rich in terms of sharing in the life of God's kingdom, a kingdom that will have no end. Jesus left his eternal home in order that we might share that home with him. Compared to this, all else is but nothing.

Paul had been talking about money. He was in fact challenging the Corinthians to be more generous in their giving. He cited the Christians of Macedonia who gave not only what they could, but more than they could. This leads him then to speak of Jesus. In the words of Eugene Peterson's *The Message*: 'You are familiar with the generosity of our Master, Jesus Christ. Rich as he was, he gave it all

---

4. Quoted by Robert Andrews (ed.), *Collins Thematic Dictionary of Quotations* (London: HarperCollins, 2nd ed., 1992), p. 205.

5. Quoted by J. Potter Briscoe (ed.), *Sydney Smith: His Wit and Wisdom* (London, 1900), p. 89.

away for us – in one stroke he became poor and we became rich.' Such a text calls for reflection.

Jesus was 'rich'. Here we have a reminder that Jesus did not begin his life when he was born in Bethlehem. His thirty-three years on earth were but a brief interlude between two eternities. Before his incarnation Jesus as the Son of God shared his Father's glory. Thus, on the eve of his passion, Jesus prayed in the garden of Gethsemane: 'So now, Father, glorify me in your own presence with the glory that I had in your presence before the world existed' (John 17:5). The deepest and most important fact about the nativity is that it was not just the birth of a child, but rather the incarnation of the Word, who was from all eternity. The child in his manger bed is the Eternal Son who before all the worlds were made is one with the Father. Jesus is the Word made flesh; in him we see what God is truly like.

A story is told of a traveller in Finland who spent a day in the midst of some sublime scenery, with lofty mountains and mighty forests. But he returned home strangely unhappy. In the living room of the house where he was staying were three canaries in a cage. When he entered, they became restless, chirping loudly, flitting from perch to perch, but when he went over and spoke to them they became quiet and contented. In that room there was also a small dog whining. When the traveller sat down, the dog came and pawed at his knee and there was a look on his face that said, 'Are you never going to notice me?' The man spoke and patted the dog, whereupon he too was content. 'Then I knew why all that day I myself had been restless. I had felt God in nature, but I wanted something more. I wanted to be noticed. I wanted a word, a touch.' The good news of Christmas is that God has noticed us: he has come to us in Jesus; he has spoken to us in his Son; he has reached out and touched us.

Jesus became poor. He knew poverty at birth: not for him a cradle in a king's palace, but rather, his bed was a feeding trough. He knew poverty as he grew up. The lack of references to Joseph in the later Gospel stories may well suggest that Joseph died at an early age, with the result that Jesus, as the eldest, may have had to be the breadwinner and thus had to care for his mother and his siblings. If this was so, then he would have had no easy home life. It could well have been that it was this need to support his family that caused him to wait until he was thirty before he began his ministry. Furthermore, he knew poverty in his ministry. For Jesus enjoyed no great financial package as he went about preaching and teaching and doing good. To one would-be follower Jesus declared: 'Foxes have holes, and birds of the air have nests; but the Son of Man has nowhere to lay his head' (Luke 9:58). He knew poverty too at death. It was perhaps not by chance that when Jesus died, he was laid in a tomb belonging to another. Yes, from the beginning to the end of his short life Jesus knew what it was to be poor.

But the emphasis here is on a metaphorical, metaphysical poverty. In this respect Philippians 2:6 is a good parallel. Jesus 'though he was in the form of God, did not regard equality with God as something to be exploited, but emptied himself'. That is, Jesus, the Lord of glory, emptied himself of all but love. What did this involve? It involved laying aside his omnipotence: Creator of all, he became like one of his creatures. In the words of the writer to the Hebrews, 'He had to become like his brothers and sisters in every respect' (Heb. 2:17). Yes, he went around doing many mighty works, but these he did in the power of the Spirit, the same Spirit who is available to us. He also laid aside his divine omniscience. Therefore, Luke could write: 'Jesus increased in wisdom and in years, and in divine and human favour' (Luke 2:52). There were things Jesus did not know. Thus, speaking of the day when God will wind up all human history, he could say: 'But about that day or hour no one knows, neither the angels in heaven, nor the Son, but only the Father' (Mark 13:32). He even laid aside his immortality: 'Jesus . . . for a little while was made lower than the angels . . . so that by the grace of God he might taste death for everyone' (Heb. 2:9). Jesus, who shared in the creative life-giving activity of God, gave his life a ransom for many. At this point the Lord of glory plumbed the absolute depths: 'And being found in human form, he humbled himself and became obedient to the point of death – even death on a cross' (Phil. 2:7–8). If we were to graph it, we would have to draw the line going down, down, down and down. To say that Jesus became poor is indeed an understatement!

But it was 'for our sakes' that he became poor! The manger-cradle, the cruel pinch of poverty, the poisoned hate of enemies, the agony of the garden, the bitter cross, the dark grave – Jesus bore them all for one great end: 'for our sakes'.

It has been said that the difference between a sermon and a lecture is that a sermon is addressed to individuals, has a personal quality and asks: 'How does this matter concern you?' At this point the preacher can be direct and say: 'Well, let me be personal. Has Jesus enriched you? Do you know what it is to begin to experience in Jesus something of the life of God? Have you yet to receive the free gift of life and love that God offers to each one of us in his Son? Have you yet to discover the true Christmas jackpot that is freely offered to you?'

God's timing is always right (Gal. 4:4–5)

But when the fullness of time had come, God sent his own Son, born of a woman, born under the law, in order to redeem those who were under the law, so that we might receive adoption as children.

God's timing

God's timing is always spot on. And nowhere more do we see this than when it came to the coming of Jesus into this world. Jesus came at 'the right time' (GNB); 'When the fullness of time had come, God sent his Son'. Nobody can claim to know what was in God's mind. Nonetheless, from a human perspective at least, we can deduce a number of factors that may well have involved the time being right.

First, the time was right because the Roman Empire had reached its peak. Rome had conquered and subdued the known, inhabited world. And in conquering and subduing this world, Rome had built its roads. These roads were built for the easy movement of troops, but in God's providence they facilitated the spread of the gospel. Jesus may have been born in a Roman backwater: Nazareth and Bethlehem were far from being household words in the Roman world. Nevertheless, thanks to the Roman communications system, this babe of Bethlehem, this Jesus of Nazareth, became a household word within a century or two.

The time was also right because Greek had become the common language ('lingua franca') of the Roman Empire. The Roman Empire was composed of many nations and many tongues. In order to trade, a common language was needed: thanks to the exploits of Alexander the Great, the language chosen was not Latin, but Greek. This common language of Greek facilitated the spread of the gospel and, probably more than anything else, enabled the Christian gospel to break out from the narrow confines of Judaism and become the faith for everyone.

The time was right because there was a hunger for God. The old mythological gods of Greece and Rome were losing their hold on the common people. Nobody really believed in the gods who frolicked on Mount Olympus. People were looking for a religion that was real and satisfying. This was the time of the growth of the 'mystery' religions, which talked of personal salvation. But even these popular mystery religions failed to satisfy. For they too were mythological: the gods they worshipped died and rose each year. This was also the time when many non-Jews were attracted to the lofty ideals of Judaism. Into this world where people hungered for spiritual reality God sent his Son.

The time was right because the Jewish law had done its work in preparing for the coming of Jesus. We Christians must never forget that Jesus cannot be understood apart from the Old Testament. He is the Messiah, the one whom the Jews had long awaited. But by the time Jesus came, the Jewish religion had reached its sell-by date. It had become a negative rather than a positive force. It had become burdensome rather than life-enhancing. It was very much 'the right time' when God sent his Son.

God's Son became one with us

God's Son became one with us by being 'born of a woman'. At first sight this phrase may seem to allude to the virgin birth, but Paul was simply using a common Jewish idiom to say that Jesus was truly human. We find the same idiom on the lips of Jesus when he said of John the Baptist: 'Truly I tell you, among those born of women no one has arisen greater than John the Baptist' (Matt. 11:11; see Luke 7:28). However, the fact that there is no reference to the virgin birth here does not make Paul's statement any less staggering. For the wonder of the birth of Jesus is not 'how' he came, but 'that' he came. Jesus, the Son of God, who had from all eternity been sharing in the life of God, was 'born of a woman' and in so doing shared our human experience.

A year or so ago I was one of the invited guests to witness one of the royals opening a new building. But although the prince visited our town that day, in no way did he identify with the ordinary people. After all, this was a royal visit. He may have shaken a few hands, but he did not mingle with the crowd. His time was spent with the important people. His visit bore no relationship to the time when Jesus visited our earth. Indeed, 'visit' is the wrong word to describe the coming of Jesus among us. He was 'born of a woman'; he became a man of flesh and blood, a man like us. In the words of one commentator: 'He was vulnerable to all the conditions of human life which constantly threaten and unsettle – fear, loneliness, suffering, temptation, doubt and ultimately godforsakeness.'[6]

God's Son was also 'born under the law'. In this particular context, where Paul is arguing about the place of the Jewish law, Paul is concerned to point out that Jesus was a Jew and as such was subject to the Jewish law. Jesus knew what it was like to submit to all the requirements of the Jewish law. What is more, Jesus went on to succeed where all others failed: for Jesus lived a life of perfect obedience to the law of God. When Jesus in the Sermon on the Mount spoke of a 'righteousness' exceeding that of the scribes and the Pharisees (Matt. 5:20), he knew what he was talking about. In a way that was true of no other, Jesus 'fulfilled' the law and the prophets (Matt. 5:17). In this respect Jesus was different from us. For although one of us, his sinlessness sets him apart from us. It was, however, precisely this combination of humanity and perfection that qualified him to become the Saviour of the world. Jesus, was able to offer that one perfect sacrifice to God. As Paul later wrote to the Corinthians: 'For our sake he [God] made him [Christ] to be sin who knew no sin, so that in him we might become the righteousness of God' (2 Cor. 5:21).

Incidentally, we should notice that from first to last salvation is a work of God. It was 'God' who 'sent his Son'. Jesus did not set out to provide a way of salvation. Rather, it was God who took the initiative and sent his Son to our world. This fact is well illustrated by an unusual picture hanging in an Italian church. At first glance it is like

---

6. Charles B. Cousar, *Galatians*, Interpretation Commentary (Atlanta: John Knox Press, 1982), p. 94.

any other painting of the cross. But, as we look more closely, we perceive there is a difference, because 'there's a vast shadowy Figure behind the figure of Jesus. The nail that pierces the hand of Jesus goes through the hand of God. The spear thrust into the side of Jesus goes through God's side.'[7]

God's purpose in our freedom

The purpose for God's saving initiative was twofold – the one negative, the other positive.

Expressed negatively, it was 'to redeem those who were under the law'. Jesus came to free those who were in bondage to the law, and he did so by paying a ransom. Today, thanks to hijackings and kidnappings, we have become familiar with the concept of a ransom price. Money is paid, or a deal is struck, which enables those captured to go free. In Paul's day there were no hijackings or kidnappings, but the concept of ransom money was a common one. For favoured slaves could be set free by the paying of a ransom price. It is this image of freedom from slavery that is present here. God sent his Son to die on the cross that we might be free.

Now elsewhere in Paul's writings the freedom that he has in mind is freedom from sin. But here the emphasis is on freedom from 'law': that is, freedom from religion. In the previous chapter Paul wrote: 'Now before faith came, we were imprisoned and guarded under the law until faith would be revealed' (Gal. 3:23). At Mount Sinai God gave to Moses the Ten Commandments for the good of the people. But over the years the law had become more refined and more complicated. The scribes had added all kinds of rules and regulations, with the laudable intention of enabling people to fulfil the law better; but the intention had been counter-productive. The law had become a burden; so much so, that it had, in effect, enslaved people into a deadly form of religiosity. What was true of the law has been true of religion in general. Alas, all too often religion, far from being a liberating force, has become a narrowing, enslaving one.

That was Martin Luther's experience before his conversion. For a scrupulously conscientious monk, who spent hour after hour in

---

7. George Buttrick.

prayer, religion was a burden rather than a joy. Instead of loving God, he feared God.

That was also John Wesley's experience before his heart was 'strangely warmed'. As an Oxford undergraduate he was into religion in a big way: he and his friends formed a so-called Holy Club that centred upon the minutiae of religious observance (hence the name of 'Methodist'); but it was all method, and no Spirit. As Wesley later wrote, 'I had then only the faith of a servant, not that of a son.'[8]

Some of us can think back to childhoods that were dominated by a similar dreadful form of religious negativity: alcohol was sinful, so too dancing and chewing gum! On holiday enjoying yourself on a Sunday was sinful: you couldn't go to the beach, couldn't swim or build sandcastles. It was a soul-destroying form of Christian religion. But Jesus came to set us free from religion and all its life-denying side effects: 'God sent his own Son . . . to redeem those who were under the law'.

The price Jesus paid was a life of total obedience offered up to God on a cross. So Paul writes in Galatians 3:13: 'Christ redeemed us from the curse of the law by becoming a curse for us – for it is written, "Cursed is everyone who hangs on a tree"'. From now on, faith – and faith alone – is the means by which we may be put right with God.

Expressed positively, 'God sent his own Son . . . so that we might receive adoption as children'. What an amazing thought that we can become God's sons and daughters; or it is amazing to those who come to the Christian faith with fresh eyes. The trouble with us is that we have lost our sense of wonder. Many years ago a Danish Mission in India appointed some of its Indian converts to translate their catechism. A catechism was a training manual normally used by confirmation candidates, which consists of questions and answers. One question asked what the supreme privilege of Christians was, to which the answer was: 'To be called the children of God.' One of the Indian translators was startled at so bold a saying. It seemed too good to be true: 'It is too much!' he said. 'Let me rather render it, "They shall be permitted to kiss his feet."'

The good news is that God wants us to be called his children. God

---

8. John Wesley, *Journal*, I (London, 1872), p. 76n.

wants us to enter an intimate relationship with him, whereby we can call him 'Abba, Father'. But God in his love never forces his gifts of love on us: they are always there for the taking. We need to stretch out the hand of faith and take the Lord Jesus as our own personal Saviour. We do this as we, with Paul, say 'the Son of God . . . loved me and gave himself for me' (Gal. 2:20); at that point we may know the freedom of the children of God for ourselves!

Jesus the servant-king (Phil. 2:6–11)

[Let the same mind be in you that was in Christ Jesus,]

who, though he was in the form of God,
  did not regard equality with God
  as something to be exploited,
but emptied himself,
  taking the form of a slave,
  being born in human likeness.
And being found in human form,
  he humbled himself
  and became obedient to the point of death –
  even death on a cross.

Therefore God also highly exalted him
  and gave him the name
  that is above every name,
so that at the name of Jesus
  every knee should bend,
  in heaven and on earth and under the earth,
and every tongue should confess
  that Jesus Christ is Lord,
  to the glory of God the Father.

The wonder of the Christmas story is well expressed in the Christ-hymn of Philippians 2. Here we see that the birth of Jesus in the manger was but one step on a path of six steps or stages that led from eternity to a cross and on to glory.

Stage 1: God from all eternity

'He was in the form of God' (2:6), or as other versions express it, 'He always had the nature of God' (GNB), 'the divine nature was his from the first' (NEB). Right from the very beginning Christians have affirmed that Jesus was the Son of God. He was no ordinary man. From all eternity he shared in the very being of God. In the words of the fourth-century Nicene Creed: 'We believe in one Lord, Jesus Christ, the only Son of God, eternally begotten of the Father, God from God, Light from Light, true God from true God, begotten, not made, of one Being with the Father'. It is not easy to get our minds around this concept of Christ's 'pre-existence': we are dealing with something beyond our experience and that defies all human understanding. But God's ways are not our ways (Isa. 55:8). The very fact that we are dealing with mystery, is a sign we are dealing with God. The truth is that if faith no longer defied all human logic, God would no longer be God.

The hymn goes on: 'he did not regard equality with God as something to be exploited' (2:6). That is, although the divine nature was his, Jesus did not seek the status that God the Father alone enjoys as ruler of the universe. We should note that there is a very real difference between 'nature' and 'status'. Children share their parents' nature but not their status. They are what we are, in that they are our 'flesh and blood'; what we are, they are. But there is a distinction between us: we are their parents; they are our children. Similarly, there is a distinction within the Godhead: the Son is subordinate to the Father. Though Jesus shared in the nature of God, unlike Adam he did not seek to make himself equal with God.

Stage 2: Glory laid aside

'But [he] emptied himself, taking the form of a slave' (2:7). Or as other versions put it, Jesus 'gave up all he had' (GNB), 'he made himself nothing' (REB). What did he give away? Of what did he empty himself? How did he make himself nothing? Jesus gave up his glory, and thus 'stripped himself of the insignia of his majesty'.[9]

---

9. J. B. Lightfoot, St Paul's Epistle to the Philippians (London: Macmillan, 1913), p. 112.

In becoming one with us, Jesus limited himself by subjecting himself to a number of 'disciplines'. He shared with us the discipline of space. From the manger to the tomb, Jesus accepted the physical restrictions of this life; we may talk of the 'omnipresence' of God, but not of the Jesus of history. Jesus could only be at one place at a time. Jesus accepted the physical restrictions of being an ordinary Palestinian Jew. Apart from his evacuation as a baby to Egypt, there is no evidence that he ever left the Holy Land. He shared with us the discipline of time. For the Eternal God a thousand years may be but as a day, but for the Jesus of history a day was made up of but twenty-four hours, with each hour composed of but sixty minutes. Jesus knew what it was like to work against the clock; indeed, his whole ministry had to be compressed within the space of thirty months or so. He shared with us the discipline of 'ignorance', in the sense that Jesus did not know everything. God the Father may be 'omniscient' and know all things, but not the Jesus of history. True, Jesus had special insights, both into the character of others as also into the character of God. Yet he remained limited. He did not know, for instance, the day or the hour when the world would end. Jesus, for our salvation, 'emptied himself'. What an amazing act of service! It almost beggars belief that the Son of God could love us so.

Stage 3: Like and yet not like us

'Taking the form of a slave, being born in human likeness', Jesus became one with us, one of us. Only so could he save us. For as the writer to the Hebrews put it: 'he had to become like his brothers and sisters in every respect, so that he might be a merciful and faithful high priest in the service of God, to make a sacrifice of atonement for the sins of the people' (Heb. 2:17).

Jesus did not pretend to be a man: he was a man. He shared our flesh and blood. When they plunged a spear into his side, he bled like any of us would have bled. He experienced all the emotions we experience. He knew what it was like to be angry and frustrated, to be sad and to be happy. Jesus was truly man, and not merely man. Yet Jesus was more than a man. He was 'born in human likeness'. There is a degree of ambiguity in this statement, emphasizing that he was similar to our humanity in some respects and dissimilar in others: the similarity lies with his full humanity; the dissimilarity in that he was not 'human' only. 'He was God living out a truly human life.'[10]

Stage 4: Obedient to death

Jesus lived no ordinary life. Jesus, who took 'the form of a slave' (2:7), lived a life of 'obedient' service. Jesus first accepted the discipline of obedient service when he was baptized by John the Baptist. His parents may have dedicated him to the Lord when they presented him in the temple to Simeon, but Jesus dedicated himself to God's service when he presented himself to John the Baptist at the river Jordan. John hesitated to baptize him, but Jesus replied: 'It is proper for us in this way to fulfil all righteousness' (Matt. 3:15). There, at the very beginning of his ministry, Jesus took the first step of obedience that was to lead to the cross. This discipline of obedient service characterized the whole of his ministry. Jesus could have listened to Peter, who when Jesus spoke of his impending death, cried out: 'God forbid it, Lord! This must never happen to you!' (Matt. 16:22). Right up until the end, Jesus could have saved his skin and backed out of confrontation with the religious leaders of his day. But, as it was, he consciously and deliberately set his face to go God's way, whatever the cost might be. This discipline of obedient service climaxed in his death on a cross.

This obedience led Jesus even to 'death on a cross'. The cross was reserved for slaves and for so-called terrorists. No-one in the first century wore a cross as a medallion around his or her neck. It was a symbol of torture and degradation. But Jesus obediently went the way of the cross. In the UK the highest honour a soldier can be awarded is the Victoria Cross; the VC is given where valour has been shown 'beyond the normal call of duty'. Jesus, for our sakes, went beyond what might reasonably have been demanded of him. In the words of one scholar: 'His obedience was a sure token of his death and his authority, for only a divine being can accept death as obedience; for ordinary men it is a necessity.'[11]

---

10. Gordon D. Fee, *Philippians* (Leicester: IVP, 1999), p. 96.

11. Ernst Lohmeyer, *Der Brief an die Philipper* (Göttingen, 9th ed., 1953), p. 195, my translation.

Stage 5: Exalted to God's right hand

Up until now Jesus has been the subject of this Christ-hymn. He it is who acts, relinquishing claims, emptying himself of his glory, becoming human, serving, obeying, dying. But now it is God who acts, raising Jesus from the dead and exalting him to his right hand. This was the Father's 'Amen' to the Son's 'It is finished'!

Let us notice too the change of key. Jesus, who has been descending into the depths, is now raised to the heights. Literally, the hymn declares that God has 'more than exalted' (*hyperypsōsen*) Jesus. The implication is that Jesus has been exalted to a higher position than he had previously enjoyed. That is, the equality at which Jesus had refused to grasp is now his. For God has given him a new name, 'the name that is greater than any other name'. This name of 'Lord' is more than a title: it denotes a new status. In Jewish thinking, a name expressed the nature of the person to whom it is attached: 'as his name is, so is he' (1 Sam. 25:25). Abram (exalted father), for instance, became Abraham (father of a multitude). Jesus, the Saviour, becomes Jesus, the Lord. He is Lord, not just in name, but in reality!

Stage 6: Lord of all

The ascension is here likened to an enthronement ceremony. Just as Queen Elizabeth II was crowned on 3 June 1953, so Jesus was crowned Lord of all when God raised him from the dead and exalted him to his right hand. Just as the Queen at her coronation was acclaimed by all, so too Jesus is acclaimed:

> So that at the name of Jesus
>   every knee should bend,
>   in heaven and on earth and under the earth,
>   and ever tongue should confess
>   that Jesus Christ is Lord,
>   to the glory of God the Father. (2:11)

What a wonderful vision, a vision of the whole universe acknowledging the lordship of Jesus. What's more, this cosmic vision involves not just all of humanity, but the spirit forces of the universe: forces not just for good, but forces also for evil. Whoever, whatever these beings may be, 'all . . . will fall on their knees, and all will openly proclaim that Jesus Christ is Lord' (2:10–11, GNB).

But it is more than a vision of the future – the hymn uses a past tense – it speaks of a process that has already begun. And that is true, is it not? Down through the centuries and across the continents, already many millions have bowed the knee. Indeed, even at this very moment there are millions of people singing the praises of Jesus. But one day every knee will have to bow; every tongue will have to confess that Jesus is Lord.

Jesus the king of creation (Col. 1:15–17)

He is the image of the invisible God, the firstborn of all creation; for in him all things in heaven and on earth were created, things visible and invisible, whether thrones or dominions or rulers or powers – all things have been created through him and for him. He himself is before all things, and in him all things hold together.

Here in the opening verses of the Christ-hymn a series of staggering affirmations are made about Jesus, the one whose birth we celebrate at Christmas.

Jesus as the image of God shares in the reign of God
First, 'He is the image of the invisible God' (1:15a). The Greek word underlying 'image' is *eikōn*, from which we get our word 'icon'. It means a 'precise copy', and was used of the head of a king on a coin, or of the statue of a famous man. So the GNB translates this phrase: 'Christ is the visible likeness of the invisible God'. Similarly, in 2 Corinthians 4:4, 6 Paul describes Christ as 'the exact likeness (*eikōn*) of God' (v. 4, GNB); 'For it is the God who said, "Let light shine out of darkness", who has shone in our hearts to give the light of the knowledge of the glory of God in the face of Jesus Christ' (v. 6). The same thought can be paralleled elsewhere in Scripture, not least in John's Gospel: 'No one has ever seen God. It is God the only Son, who is close to the Father's heart, who has made him known' (John 1:18); 'Whoever has seen me has seen the Father' (John 14:9). In other words, Jesus is no mere prophet with a message from God: 'he is the

objectivisation of God in human life'.[12] If we want to see God, then we must look at Jesus.

It is possible that we also have here an allusion to Genesis 1:26, where God says: 'Let us make humankind in our image (Septuagint: *eikōn*), according to our likeness; and let them have dominion over the fish of the sea, and over the birds of the air, and over the cattle, and over all the earth [marginal reading], and over every creeping thing that creeps upon the earth.' If so, then the idea is present that Jesus as 'the image of the invisible God' shares too in the reign of God. In other words, Jesus is the king of creation!

Jesus as God's 'firstborn' rules over all

Secondly, he is 'the firstborn of all creation' (1:15b). This apparently innocuous phrase has been the subject of theological battles down through the centuries. Thus in the fourth-century theological duel between Arius and Athanasius, Colossians 1:15 was one of the key texts. For Arius believed that this phrase pointed to Jesus not being truly part of the Godhead: he was but a creature, albeit a perfect creature. This point of view is, of course, today maintained by Jehovah's Witnesses. Taken quite literally, and interpreted without reference to the context, it is true that this phrase could quite possibly be given the Arian sense of Christ's being included among the created things. That is, Christ was not there with the Father from all eternity; he came on to the scene a little later, as a result of the Father's creative activity. But in biblical interpretation it is always dangerous to isolate a phrase without reference to its setting: 'a text without a context is a pretext'. This is true here. For an Arian interpretation is inconsistent with the declaration of verse 16, where 'all things [not 'the rest'] have been created through him'. Christ is not to be included among the created order. In the words of Athanasius: 'But if all creatures were created in him, he is other than the creatures, and he is not a creature but the creator of his creatures.' As the firstborn, Jesus is the firstborn before creation: as firstborn, Christ is before all things.

But almost certainly this affirmation is not first and foremost

---

12. Ralph Martin, *Colossians and Philemon*, New Century Bible (London: Marshall, Morgan & Scott, 1974), p. 57.

about Christ's temporal priority. Rather, Christ's pre-existence is primarily a symbol of his pre-eminence. In this respect the story of Esau and Jacob comes to mind, in which Jacob by deceit robs his brother of his birthright: that is, he receives the blessing of the firstborn from his father Jacob:

> Let peoples serve you,
>> and nations bow down to you.
> Be lord over your brothers,
>> and may your mother's sons bow down to you. (Gen. 27:29)

Christ as the 'firstborn of all creation' (Col. 1:15) is the one who has authority over all creation. So the GNB translates this phrase: 'He is the first-born Son, superior to all created things'. In other words, Jesus is the king of creation!

Jesus as the mediator of creation is Lord of all

The hymn declares: 'for in him all things in heaven and on earth were created, things visible and invisible, whether thrones or dominions or rulers or powers' (1:16). The point here is that the whole world belongs to him because he made it. It is his by right. This was a revolutionary statement. Revolutionary in the sense that it reduced the evil powers, which so worried first-century men and women, to their proper dimensions: even they owed their existence to him. As G. H. C. Macgregor once put it: 'Having been "created in him" they are essentially subject powers, so that even their hostility is compelled to subserve God's plan.'[13]

The hymn goes on: 'all things have been created through him and for him'. This is more than a restatement of what has been said. For Jesus is here described not only as the mediator of God's work in creation, but also the goal of all creation. In other words, all things were created to find their focal point in him.

There is another point of interest. Although the English translations give the impression that the same verb is used twice in the same

---

13. G. H. C. Macgregor. 'Principalities and Powers: The Cosmic Background of Paul's Thought', *New Testament Studies* 1 (1954–5), pp. 17–28.

tense in verse 16, this is not the case. In verse 16a where the reference is to all things being created in him, the aorist tense is used – a one-off action is implied that is already in the past, whereas in verse 16d we have the perfect tense: a past action is carried over into the present. The hymn is probably not so much concerned to propound an evolutionary view of creation, as to say that the creation has a permanent and indissoluble relationship to Christ, a relationship that ever seeks to find fulfilment in him.

Jesus as the sustainer of creation is supreme over all

As with the phrase 'firstborn of all creation', so the assertion that Jesus 'is before all things' (1:17) is above all a statement of supremacy over all things. Otherwise the imperfect tense ('he was') would have been expected. As the one before all things, Jesus is supreme.

This idea of supremacy comes also in the claim that 'in him all things hold together'. The underlying Greek word was often used by the Stoics to describe the 'binding together' of the universe: in other words, Jesus is described as the cohesive principle of power in the universe. The same thought is found in Hebrews 1:3 (RSV), where Christ is described as 'upholding the universe by his word of power'. However, as with the proposition that Christ is the agent of creation, so here what is being propounded is not a particular cosmological theory but rather a theological affirmation: Jesus is the king of creation, who not only set the universe in motion at the beginning of time, but who is also responsible for all that has appeared since then. In the words of Ralph Martin, 'no new cosmic force can take him by surprise and no power which arises subsequent to the first creation "in the beginning" can usurp this right'. What a thought. Jesus is more than a constitutional monarch, holding simply vestigial powers. As the ongoing sustainer, he alone is supreme.

Jesus the saviour (Titus 2:11)

the grace of God has appeared, bringing salvation to all . . .

Here in this one verse we have the gospel in a nutshell. Jesus is God's grace personified (see also 2 Tim. 1:9)!

Light shines

When all is dark around, what a difference light makes. On those rare occasions when a power cut strikes and even the street lighting goes off, it can be scary finding our way home: especially if the clouds have hidden the moon and stars from our view. We need light to find our way about. In that context Paul writes: 'the grace of God has appeared'. Or, in the words of the NEB/REB, 'the grace of God has dawned'.

The verb present here (*epiphaneō*) is found in Luke 1:78–79, where Zechariah proclaims:

> By the tender mercy of our God,
>> the dawn from on high will break upon us,
> to give light to those who sit in darkness and in
>> the shadow of death,
>> to guide our feet into the way of peace.

Zechariah's picture here is of a world in darkness, in which people have lost their sense of direction. It is a world without purpose, without joy, and without peace. Zechariah's world is also our world. People may celebrate the season of Christmas with music and dancing in pubs and clubs, but their celebrations are hollow and meaningless, and are reminiscent of the dance band playing as the *Titanic* sank. For without Christ we are lost and doomed to a Godless eternity.

Against such a backdrop Paul declares: 'the grace of God has appeared'. At a particular moment in history, God in his grace entered our world in the person of his Son to dispel the darkness.

Jesus saves

But there is another picture present. For the underlying Greek word, from which we get our word 'epiphany', was used not just of the appearing of light, but of the appearing of a Saviour. For instance, in the book of 2 Maccabees, a Hellenistic text from the first century BC, which is part of the Apocrypha, Israel is saved from her enemies by an 'appearance' (*epiphaneia*) of God: so Heliodorus, who threatened to plunder the temple of its treasures, was overcome by an 'appearance' of the 'Lord of Spirits and the Prince of Power' (2 Maccabees

3:24–30); similarly, the slaughter of some 35,000 men by Maccabeus and his small army is attributed to an 'appearance' of God (2 Maccabees 15:22–27). The same word was used of the saving appearance of a pagan god. For instance, there were dozens of temples devoted to the worship of Asclepius, the god of healing: Asclepius was said to have brought about many cures through his 'appearances'. The same word was also used in the developing cult of emperor worship: such occasions as the birth or enthronement or victory of an emperor could be called an 'epiphany'. One temple inscription found in Ephesus speaks of Julius Caesar as 'god made manifest (*epiphanies*), born of Ares and Aphrodite, the common saviour of human life'.

In such a context, Paul declares that 'the grace of God has appeared, bringing salvation to all'. When Jesus was born in Bethlehem, God in his grace intervened to save us from our sin.

No expense spared

Salvation is God's Christmas gift to the world. It is a gift where no expense was spared. For God has given us his all. The story is told of a minister talking to a couple who were having difficulties in their marriage. There was much bitterness and pain, coupled with an acute lack of understanding. At one point in the exchange the husband spoke up in obvious exasperation: 'I've given you everything,' he said to his wife. 'I've given you a new home. I've given you a new car and all the clothes you can wear. I've given you . . .' And he went on to list all kinds of things. When he had ended, the wife said sadly: 'That much is true, John. You have given me everything . . . but yourself.' By contrast, God has given his very self: he has given us his Son.

Needless to say, this gift of God is a gift of grace. God is not simply a beneficent God; he is a gracious God. His giving is totally undeserved. To Cretans, as indeed to others living in a culture dominated by Greek philosophy, this message of grace was revolutionary. For, according to the Greek philosophers of that day, love for the unlovable was just not on. The Greek philosopher Aristotle once said: 'Only he who is deserving of love can be loved.' Similarly, Plato once said: 'Love is for the lovely.' But God in his grace loved us even 'while we still were sinners' (Rom. 5:8). No wonder Paul in his great paean of praise speaks of God lavishing (see Eph. 1:8) his grace upon us.

A happy Christmas to us all!

It doesn't matter who we are or what we have done, God wants us all to have a 'happy Christmas' in the deepest sense of that phrase. For God had us all in view when his saving grace appeared.

In the immediate context of our text, where Paul has just been speaking to slaves, he may have in mind that God's grace is for all, whatever our social standing. Or in a letter written to Cretans, who were a much disdained and despised group of people (see Paul's quotation of Epimenides of Knossos in Titus 1:12), Paul may have in mind that God's grace is for all, whatever our background. For, as Paul wrote to Timothy, 'God our Saviour . . . desires everyone to be saved and to come to the knowledge of the truth' (1 Tim. 2:3–4). There are no limits to the saving grace of God. The love of God, which stooped in Bethlehem and embraced us all at Calvary is able to deal with the worst of sinners. Jesus, said John, 'is the atoning sacrifice . . . for the sins of the whole world' (1 John 2:2). The 'breadth and length and height and depth' of the love of Christ truly surpass all knowledge and understanding (Eph. 3:18–19).

Yes please – No thank you!

God has taken the initiative and has loved us beyond our deserving. He now awaits our response. In the first place, we must respond in faith. We must say 'Yes' to God, and we do this as we give ourselves back to him in love and gratitude. Grace, it has been said, means 'all of him for me'; and faith means 'all of me for him'.

But as well as saying 'Yes' to God and his grace, we must also say 'No' to this world and its values. For we cannot accept Jesus as our Saviour without at the same time making him Lord of our lives. The grace of God has appeared not only to bring us salvation, but to train us to 'renounce impiety and worldly passions, and . . . to live lives that are self-controlled, upright, and godly' (Titus 2:12). Grace may be free, but it is never cheap! The words of Bonhoeffer are, alas, as relevant as ever:

> Cheap grace is the deadly enemy of the Church. We are fighting today for

costly grace . . . Cheap grace is the preaching of forgiveness without requiring repentance, baptism without Church discipline, Communion without confession, absolution without personal confession. Cheap grace is grace without discipleship, grace without the Cross.[14]

Jesus the Word of God (Heb. 1:1–3)

Long ago God spoke to our ancestors in many and various ways by the prophets. But in these last days he has spoken to us by a Son, whom he appointed heir of all things, through whom he also created the world. He is the reflection of God's glory and the exact imprint of God's very being, and he sustains all things by his powerful word. When he had made purification for sins, he sat down at the right hand of the Majesty on high.

Even today most people in the UK still believe in God. But what sort of God do they believe in? According to one nationwide survey, 37% think of God as a person, while 42% think of God as some impersonal force or power. But even that doesn't tell us much. It would, for instance, be interesting to know how the 37% would answer the question 'What sort of a person is God?'

The fact is that, left to our imagination and speculation, all sorts of weird ideas emerge as to the nature of God. But the good news is that we are not left to ourselves. God is not the subject of guesswork. God has spoken, and in speaking he has shown what kind of God he is.

God first spoke through the prophets

Initially God spoke 'by the prophets' (1:1). When the writer to the Hebrews refers to the prophets, he is not just thinking of the prophets featured in the second half of the Old Testament; for people like Moses, Samuel and Elijah were also regarded as prophets. No, the whole of the Old Testament is a record of God's self-revelation, a record of God's speaking to his people about himself.

---

14. Dietrich Bonhoeffer, *The Cost of Discipleship* (ET London: SCM Press, 1959), pp. 35–36.

Our text recognizes that there was no one way in which God spoke: God spoke 'in many and various ways'. On the one hand, he spoke in the storm and thunder to Moses; yet on the other hand he spoke in a still small voice to Elijah. God spoke to some through extraordinary visions, dreams and signs. Yet God also spoke to others through their ordinary everyday experiences of life; while to others again he spoke into the innermost recesses of their minds and hearts, as they wrestled with the issues of the day.

But in speaking to the prophets, God did not reveal all of himself. God did not speak fully. The clear implication of this opening verse is that 'until the coming of God the revelation of God remained incomplete'.[15] This comes out very clearly in the translation adopted by the NEB: 'he spoke in fragmentary and varied fashion through the prophets'. Or as the Living Bible paraphrase renders it: 'Long ago God spoke in many different ways to our fathers through the prophets . . . telling them little by little about his plans'. We see this fragmentary nature of God's revelation perhaps in the way in which the prophets are often characterized by one dominant idea. For example, Amos is essentially one long cry for social justice; Isaiah, as a result of his vision of God in the temple, is dominated by the idea of the holiness of God; Hosea, because of his own bitter home experience, realizes something of the wonder of the grace of God. However, the fact that the prophets' understanding of God was fragmentary and partial should not lead us to despise or underrate their words. The Old Testament may not contain the whole truth, but it does contain truth: truth concerning the nature of God that is still of utmost significance and relevance. In the Old Testament we do not see the idea of God gradually evolving, in the sense that the prophets gradually came nearer and nearer the truth. Rather, the Old Testament is the story of God's progressive revelation; at each stage truth was present, but it was not the whole story.

God has now spoken through the person of his Son

What was only in part revealed through the prophets is now fully

---

15. William L. Lane, *Hebrews 1–8*, Word Biblical Commentary 47a (Dallas, Texas: Word, 1991), p. 10.

revealed in Jesus Christ: 'in these last days he has spoken to us by his Son' (1:2). Jesus is God's final and fullest Word.

But how did God reveal himself? Did Jesus have more to say about God than the prophets? Clearly, the teachings of Jesus are invaluable for our understanding of the nature of God and of what God would have us to be. But if the significance of Jesus resulted solely in his teaching – was to be found only in his word – he would still be just a prophet, albeit the greatest of prophets. The importance of Jesus lies not just in what he said, but in who he was and what he did. God spoke through his very life and being. For whereas the prophets were but friends of God, Jesus was the Son of God.

The writer to the Hebrews was in no doubt that Jesus was the Son of God. God 'has spoken to us by a Son'. As the Son of God, Jesus was able to reveal the Father in a way previously unknown. We have a saying, 'like father, like son'. I am told by some who knew my father that some of my mannerisms when preaching remind them of him. It is not that I have set out to copy him. But rather, quite unconsciously, I have modelled myself on him. What is true in some small way of me and my father was all the more true of Jesus.

As the Son of God, the writer to the Hebrews declares, Jesus is 'the reflection of God's glory' (1:3; REB: 'He is the radiance of God's glory'). In the Old Testament the presence of God was associated with splendour beyond imagining, the kind of splendour that makes all the pomp and circumstance of a queen's coronation or an archbishop's enthronement seem mundane. The Old Testament used the word 'glory' to describe this unimaginable splendour. For Jesus, therefore, to reflect the brightness of God's glory is to reflect the brightness of his presence. But how is Jesus able to reflect such brightness? An analogy drawn from an eclipse of the sun may help: 'As smoked glass, at the time of an eclipse, allows the safe study of the sun's "corona", so Jesus makes the divine glory bearable to human eyes: we cannot bear to gaze upon the sun's full splendour, but we can live in sunlight, shining through Jesus Christ.'[16]

As the Son of God, Jesus is also 'the exact imprint of God's very

---

16. R. E. O. White, *Sermon Suggestions in Outline* (London: Pickering & Inglis, 1965), p. 154.

being'. The underlying Greek word (*charaktēr*) was used of the impression of a stamp on a seal. The idea is of a seal impressed on wax or clay, the incut design shaping the soft material to its own reflection. So the incarnation of the Son of God reproduces God's image impressed on human clay. Just as if we look at the impression, we see exactly what the seal that made it is like, so if we look at Jesus, we see exactly what God is like. To see Jesus is to see God. In Jesus we see God's true 'character'. So the great Christ-hymn of Colossians 1 declares: 'He is the image of . . . God' (Col. 1:15). 'No one has ever seen God. It is God the only Son, who is close to the Father's heart, who has made him known' (John 1:18). What a claim to make of a man still within the living memory of many! But then, this was a claim that Jesus made of himself: 'Whoever has seen me has seen the Father' (John 14:9). Unlike any prophet or religious leader, Jesus came not just to tell us about God, but to show us God.

God has spoken through the birth, life, death and resurrection of Jesus

Here there is room for the preacher to develop the idea of the God who has revealed himself in Jesus. In the first instance, we see the glory of God in a manger. In the words of John: 'the Word became flesh . . . we have seen his glory, the glory as of a father's only son' (John 1:14). At first sight such a claim may seem paradoxical. For humanly speaking there was nothing glorious about that stable, nor was there anything glorious about a helpless, if not incontinent, baby. And yet with the eyes of faith we see the glory of God's love in human form. God has spoken; in an amazing fashion he has spoken a word of love.

We see too the glory of God in the life of Jesus as a whole: in his teaching, in his healing, in his claim to forgive people their sins. There God was at work too. So John writes that at Cana of Galilee Jesus 'revealed his glory; and his disciples believed in him' (John 2:11). For Jesus was no ordinary man – he was not even the most wonderful man who ever lived – he was (and is) the Son of God. No wonder Napoleon once said of Jesus:

> I know men; and I tell you that Jesus Christ is not a man. Superficial minds
> see a resemblance between Christ and the founders of empires, and the gods

of other religions. That resemblance does not exist. There is between
Christianity and whatever other religions the distance of infinity . . .
Everything in Christ astonishes me. His spirit overawes me, and his will
confounds me. Between him and whoever else in the world, there is no
possible term of comparison. He is truly a being by himself. His ideas and
sentiments, the truth which he announces, his manner of convincing, are not
explained either by human organization or the nature of things . . . The
nearer I approach, the more carefully I examine, everything is above me –
everything remains grand, of a grandeur which overpowers. His religion is a
revelation from an intelligence which certainly is not that of man . . . One
can absolutely find nowhere, but in him alone, the imitation of his life . . .
I search in vain in history to find the similar to Jesus Christ, or anything
which can approach the gospel. Neither history, nor humanity, nor the ages,
nor nature, offer me anything with which I am able to compare it or explain
it. Here everything is extraordinary.[17]

But above all we see the glory of God in the death and resurrection of Jesus. Yes, amazingly, God's glory was to be seen in the cross
(see John 7:39; 12:16, 23; 13:31–32). For there in the midst of evil God
was at work extending forgiveness to the sinner, bringing healing out
of pain, turning the world upside down, or better, God-side up. And
of this the resurrection was the proof. Or in the words of the writer
to the Hebrews: 'When he had made purification for sins, he sat
down at the right hand of the Majesty on high . . . crowned with
glory and honour' (1:3; 2:9).

God still speaks

The preacher, however, cannot leave it here. For the God who has
spoken in Jesus still speaks his word of love to us today. Yes, whatever
stage in life we may be at, whether we are young or old, God wants
to speak to us; and in speaking he yearns for us to respond to his love
and to enter fellowship with him. So, says the writer to the Hebrews,
'See that you do not refuse the one who is speaking' (12:25). Although
these words are in the first place addressed to a group of Jewish

---

17. Words spoken by Napoleon to a general who was visiting him in exile on St
    Helena.

Christians who were being tempted to give up their Christian faith and instead return to the faith of their fathers, they may surely be extended to all of us, whether or not we have already begun the journey of faith.

Overview: Christmas is good news for all!

For children Christmas is good news. For Christmas means parties: parties at school and parties at church, parties with friends and parties with the family, parties where there is lots to eat and games to play. Christmas also means presents: presents in a stocking and presents around a tree, presents from Father Christmas and presents from parents. And, of course, Christmas means pantomimes and nativity plays, trips to the theatre and to the cinema; even perhaps trips to the ballet and the concert hall.

Christmas is good news for adults too. For we also enjoy parties, presents and pantomimes. We love the special foods that go with Christmas, the lighting of candles and the listening to carols, and above all the being together with family and friends.

But Christmas is not good news for everybody. Christmas for many is a time of sadness and of pain. Christmas is not good news for workers, when redundancy looms; nor is it good news for families where coming together exacerbates all the old tensions. Christmas is not good news either for those who have gone through the pain of marriage breakdown, where mothers and fathers are without their children. And Christmas is not good news for those who have lost loved ones in the year that has gone by. Yes, Christmas can be bad news; it can be the time when the pain of living intensifies. The very fact that Christmas is meant to be a time of happiness only makes our unhappiness all the worse: it exposes the wound and rubs in the salt.

But the good news is that precisely for those for whom Christmas is bad news, it is in fact good news. For Jesus has come into our loneliness and pain. 'The Word became flesh' (John 1:14); Jesus shared our flesh and blood (Heb. 2:14). Jesus has entered our world and has shared our human condition. He knows what it is like to be depressed and troubled in heart, to be misunderstood by family and friends. He knows what it is to experience pain: physical pain, emotional pain, mental pain, even spiritual pain. He knows and in knowing he understands. And because he knows and understands, he can offer help and strength to those for whom life is dark and bleak.

It is against this background that a first-century Jewish Christian preacher wrote: 'Let us therefore approach the throne of grace with boldness, so that we may receive mercy and find grace to help in time of need' (Heb. 4:16). God is not unapproachable; God does not live in some ivory tower remote from human experience. For Jesus is there at his right hand, Jesus who can feel for us and with us.

Here is good news for the lonely and the weak, for those for whom life is dark and bleak. Life does not have to be lived in our own strength. For the Jesus who came is the Jesus who is ready and waiting to give help to us all. So in the words of an American paraphrase of our text: 'Let's not let it slip through our fingers . . . Let's walk right up to him and get what he is so ready to give. Take the mercy, accept the help' (Eugene Peterson, *The Message*).